LIS PALUDAN

EASY EMBROIDERY

**Translated by
Christine Crowley**

MILLS AND BOON LIMITED, LONDON

EASY EMBROIDERY
LIS PALUDAN

Edited by Per Hjort
Translated by Christine Crowley

Embroideries:
Lis Paludan
Anne Marie, aged 11 years
Pernille, aged 10 years
Elsebeth, aged 12 years
Susanne, aged 10 years
Birgitte, aged 8 years
Lars, aged 8 years
Anders, aged 6 years

Photographs:
Jes Buusmann

Drawings:
Lis Paludan
Jacob, aged 8 years
Pernille, aged 10 years

Diagrams and patterns:
Marie Louise Kilen

First published as *Eva's Broderibog*
© 1970 Fogtdals Bogforlag A/S, Copenhagen
© 1974 this edition Mills and Boon Limited,
    17-19 Foley Street, London W1A 1DR

ISBN 0 263.05428.4

Made and Printed in Great Britain
by T & A Constable Ltd
Hopetoun Street, Edinburgh

*The flower on the back cover is in
appliqué embroidery. The sections were
stuck on with Bondaweb and then
decorated with embroidery. A thin
cotton yarn was used. Stitches: buttonhole stitch, herring-bone stitch, chain
stitch, open chain stitch and French
knots. For pattern, see page 94.*

Acknowledgements

Grateful thanks must be extended to the staff of The Needlewoman Shop, Regent Street, London, W1 and to Stuart Robinson for their valuable assistance with the English edition of this book.

CONTENTS

INTRODUCTION

The time is long past when embroidery was almost automatically thought of as something needing good eyesight and much patience. In those days, many little girls were made to learn to sew fine, neat edges and to work cross stitch embroidery.

Now it is all much more fun, and we hope that this book will help as many people as possible – children and adults, girls and boys – to find out what fun it can be to work with material, needle, thread and glue, in the old way and in many other newer ways.

Indeed, embroidery need not be just a matter of following a printed line with embroidery thread of a certain quality and in certain colours. In fact anyone, by using the imagination alone, can develop his or her own patterns, colour combinations, make-up of materials and stitches.

But it is always an advantage to organize the 'craftsman' side of things. This book, therefore, includes a section giving basic ideas on how to make one's own entirely personal patterns; there are also suggestions for using simple 'home-made' patterns for various purposes.

All stitches, cords, hems, etc. are explained, with instructions and diagrams, so that anyone – even beginners – can understand them. There are same-size patterns and sewing instructions for most of the work in this book, so that you can start right away.

We hope that you will enjoy the book, whether you wish to make articles for use, decoration (there is a section with suggestions for use and mounting), or just to amuse yourself with yarns and materials – in the same way as we draw and paint on paper. The main idea behind this book is to interest you and to make you want to start.

WHAT MATERIALS AND WHAT YARNS SHALL WE USE?

In fact, anything can be used for embroidery, but when choosing your materials you must know first of all what the finished embroidery is to be used for. If you want to wash it, you must choose materials that are colour-fast and washable. If, on the other hand, you want to make a wall hanging, you can forget about soap powder and water. But there may be other circumstances that have to be considered.

On page 7 we show examples of just some of the materials used in the book. There are, of course, many other fabrics suitable for embroidery, such as felt (see pages 54 – 57), canvas, crash and scrim. Discover for yourself the exciting effects you can achieve by using different materials and yarns.

1. Calico
Calico is a cotton material and is available bleached or unbleached. It is suitable for fabric painting and printing – see the examples of potato printing and fabric painting combined with embroidery on pages 72 – 79.

2. Cotton
Cotton is available in many different qualities and colours, and is excellent for embroidery. Do not choose fabrics with too close a weave; these are more difficult to stitch. Cotton can be put to many uses: hair bands, cushions, tea cosies, wall hangings, boxes, pot holders, pin cushions, etc.

3. Hessian
Hessian is an inexpensive and versatile material. It is also available in many colours, but articles needing repeated washing or that must last for years should not be made of this material. Hessian is suitable for cushions, wall hangings, handbags, tray ribbons, table mats, etc. See the recorder case on page 23 and the wall hanging on page 41.

4. Jute aida

This is coarser than example 7 (pearl aida) and is ideal for cross stitch, holbein stitch and Rya work. The coarse weave makes it an easy material to work with. It can be used for cushions, wall hangings, runners, table mats, etc. See the steamer on page 35.

5 & 6. Linen

Linen is available in various qualities and widths. Here are just two examples: 5. (8/8) and 6. (10/10). 8/8 means that there are 8 threads to 1 cm (18/20 threads to 1 in) and 10/10 means that there are 10 threads to 1 cm (25/26 threads to 1 in). Certain qualities are also available in different colours. Linen will stand up to repeated washing and is suitable for tablecloths, napkins, wall hangings, cushions, tea cosies, etc. See the butterflies on page 24 and the trees on page 45.

7. Pearl aida

This is the finest of the aida fabrics and is particularly suitable for cross stitch, holbein stitch, Rya work, etc. It may be used for tablecloths, napkins, cushions, bookcovers, bookmarks, etc. See the train on page 34.

8. Wool

The example shown on page 7 is a worsted wool and is easy to work with. It looks very attractive when embroidered with a wool yarn, and may be used for cushions, tea cosies, wall hangings, etc. See the princess on page 39.

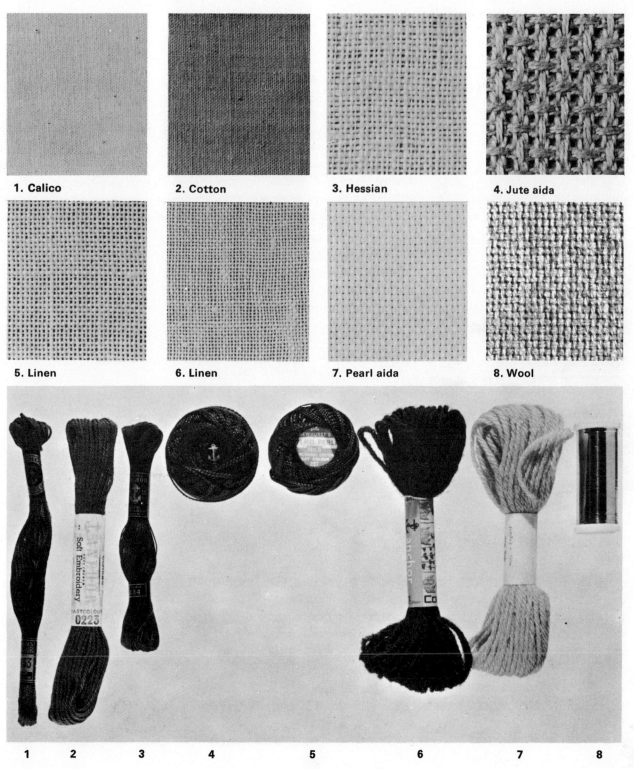

1. Calico   2. Cotton   3. Hessian   4. Jute aida

5. Linen   6. Linen   7. Pearl aida   8. Wool

1   2   3   4   5   6   7   8

What yarns?

The same applies to yarns as to fabrics; anything can be used! But here we should also think about the purpose of the embroidery – whether it should be washable, durable or merely look attractive.

Apart from the embroidery yarns shown, string, crochet and tatting cotton, darning wool, knitting wool, crewel wool, raffia or synthetic raffia, machine sewing silk, pure silk embroidery yarns, etc., may be used.

Linen yarns have been used quite a lot throughout this book, but they are not easily available in this country. However, with the wide range of colours available in the cotton yarns, this will not really matter.

1. Stranded cotton

This is a shiny, cotton yarn and has six separate strands which are loosely twisted together. It unravels easily so you can use as few or as many strands as you like. This yarn is suitable for most types of embroidery and the one shown here is called Anchor Stranded Cotton. See the picture of the girl on page 24.

2. Soft embroidery cotton

This is thicker than the stranded cotton, with a matt finish, and is particularly suitable for bold embroidery. The one shown here is called Anchor Soft Embroidery.

3. Coton à broder

This is a highly twisted, lustrous yarn. The one shown here is Anchor Coton à Broder and would look most attractive if used for the drawn thread hemstitch described on pages 92 – 93.

4 & 5. Pearl cotton

This is a smooth, corded thread. There are two thicknesses, No. 5 and No. 8. The two shown here are Anchor Pearl Cotton and Dewhurst's Sylko Perlé. You can make very attractive cords from this yarn (see page 66).

6 & 7. Embroidery wool

The two shown here are both tapestry wools which are firm and well twisted yarns. They are called Anchor Tapisserie Wool and Appleton's Tapestry Wool. See the flower embroidery on page 14 and the owl on page 42.

8. Metallic yarns

These yarns come in several different textures and thicknesses. The most popular colours are gold and silver. The one shown here is called Lurex. See the purse on page 79.

It is a good idea to have a box in which to keep bits and pieces that you might need for your embroidery work. Scraps of fabric for appliqué, buttons, sequins, string, odd lengths of yarn and knitting wool, etc., are all worth saving.

WHAT ELSE DO WE NEED?

To make an embroidery we need various items of equipment.

Needles

It is always an advantage to have a suitable selection of sewing needles in the pin cushion – thick and thin, long and short, with and without a point. For some embroidery it is best to use long needles; other work is easier with a short needle.

The needle must be suitable for the thickness of the yarn, and the eye must be large enough for easy threading.

A needle with a blunt point is good for the aida materials and other materials with a rather open weave, while a pointed needle is best for densely woven fabrics. There are instructions for pin cushions on page 84.

Scissors

You should have a large pair of scissors for cutting the fabrics and a small, pointed pair of embroidery scissors for the yarns. Never use these scissors for cutting paper, as then they will quickly become blunt.

Thimble

It is best to get used from the start to a thimble on the right middle finger. No one enjoys this at first, but it does save you some painful moments.

Adhesives

Adhesives such as Copydex or Bateman's non-flammable Rubber Paste, can be used for appliqué and felt work.

HOW DO WE BEGIN AND COMPLETE AN EMBROIDERY?

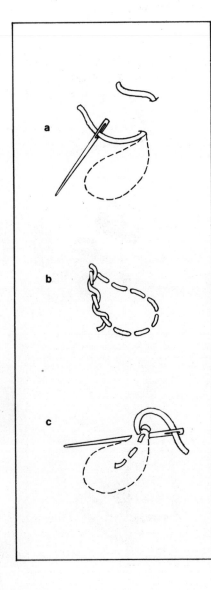

The fabric

When cutting out the fabric, it is wise to overcast the edges so that they do not fray during embroidery work.

Fastening off

a. When you begin an embroidery, it is usual to stitch into the fabric from the right side a little way from the point you wish to embroider and to leave the end of the yarn hanging down on the right side.

b. Later, when some of the embroidery has been done, the end can be 'fished' onto the reverse and fastened off (that is, secured by sewing) into the stitches on the reverse. The next time a thread is taken, the new end can be fastened into the stitches on the reverse before being brought through onto the right side. Beware of knotting the thread! You may stitch into the knot, so pulling it up onto the right side, which gives you a bulge in the embroidery.

c. Where a surface is to be covered with embroidery, the end can be fastened off by sewing with small tacking stitches beneath the places that will be covered.

→ damp pressing rag
→ rear of embroider
→ soft underlay

Pressing

d. When the embroidery work is finished it must be pressed carefully from the reverse side. Use a pressing rag for this; that is, a wet cotton rag firmly wrung. An old tea towel is perfect. Make sure that there is no dressing in the pressing rag.

To prevent the embroidery being flattened, place it on a soft underlay. This can be a thin piece of foam rubber covered with cotton or a piece of a woollen blanket. You can also make a special pressing cushion out of cotton with layers of cotton wool inside. When the embroidery has been pressed with the damp pressing rag, remove it and smooth it very lightly with a warm iron until it is dry.

TRANSFER OF PATTERNS

a

b

c

The simplest way to transfer a pattern is of course to draw it directly onto the fabric. This is done with a sharp, hard pencil. But it needs practice and some ability to draw.

At first, most people will probably prefer to start with a drawing of a pattern and transfer this to the fabric.

Transfer, using dressmaker's tracing paper

a. Place the drawing of the pattern, which must be on thin paper, such as greaseproof paper or flimsy typing paper, on the fabric and secure it with pins at the top and along the left side. Then carefully push the tracing paper beneath the pattern with the coloured side downwards. It is not advisable to fasten the tracing paper to the fabric with pins as this will leave ugly marks. Now draw over all the lines with a sharp, hard pencil or, if the pattern is a simple one, use a tracing wheel. Take care that the pattern does not shift during this and as far as possible avoid rubbing on it too much as this may leave stains on the material. As a rule the stains will disappear when washed but not all fabrics are washable.

Transparent fabric

Some fabrics are so transparent that you can see through them (for example organdie or very fine linen). They can be placed over the drawing, which is then drawn directly onto the fabric with a sharp, hard pencil.

Pricking patterns

Pricking is the classical, but perhaps the most difficult, method of tracing. b. Trace the design carefully onto tracing paper. Place the tracing on a soft underlay (a folded blanket will do) and prick holes all around the lines of the design with a darning needle. Take care to prick the holes at even intervals. The rough edges caused by the pricking on the reverse can be removed with fine sandpaper. The pattern may also be pricked on the sewing machine, using a fine needle and no thread.
Transferring the pricked pattern:
c. Place the fabric on a smooth firm underlay. Place the pricked pattern over this and secure it at the corners with something heavy.
Spread a very little 'pounce' powder (white powdered chalk or ordinary talcum powder if the fabric is dark, and black powdered charcoal if the fabric is light) onto the tracing and rub it through the holes with your finger tips or a felt pad.

When you have done this, carefully remove the tracing. Paint over the pricked lines with water colour paint and a fine brush. Use blue for light fabrics and yellow for dark fabrics.

When the paint is quite dry, give the material a brisk shake to remove the surplus powder. Do not throw the tracing away as you can use it again.

MAKE YOUR OWN DESIGNS

Anyone who can hold a pencil and who has learned to write his or her name can draw a shape. Small children need not even be able to write their own name before they can draw a house so that you can see it *is* a house. This is certainly not very difficult.

It may be difficult to decide what to draw. Shapes for embroidery work need not be particularly artistic. Quite simple designs can be brought to life by an imaginative combination of shapes, colours and materials.

On the following pages we show various suggestions which should help you get going.

See also the patterns at the back of the book.

Fill out a drawing with patterns

Try to draw a figure, for example a house, an animal or a man, or perhaps a whole landscape. Perhaps you can find an old drawing that you can use. If the drawing looks a bit dull it can be livened up by filling out the different parts with patterns, such as dots, stripes, checks, flowers or stars. It immediately becomes an entirely different picture. Look at the difference between the drawings of the boy and the houses.

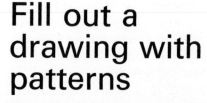

Sew in the black contours around the houses first, using back stitch. Then fill in the designs using the following stitches: stem stitch, chain stitch, herring-bone stitch, buttonhole stitch wheels, French knots and bullion knots. Page 80 shows how this embroidery of houses is made up into a cushion. For pattern, see page 101.

Free embroidery – drawing with the thread

Instead of drawing your patterns on paper and then tracing them onto the fabric, try to create embroidery directly with needle and thread. Play with the yarn, use different colours, stitches and thicknesses of yarn.

Start anywhere on the fabric, but be sure the picture is balanced so that it doesn't look lop-sided.

The drawings on the right show how a flower embroidery can come into existence. In the last-but-one drawing (e), the entire surface has been filled with small stars or dots (French knots).

There is no rule that this must be a flower picture. You could also embroider squares and fill them in so that they become houses surrounded with trees or shrubs or, as in drawing f, lots of little people. In any case it is exciting to see what will turn out when you work freely in this manner without first tracing a design.

Pattern for flower embroidery on page 99. Wool yarn in various colours has been used.

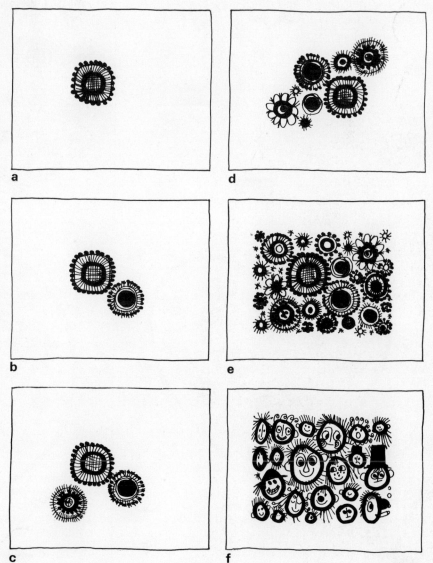

a

b

c

d

e

f

Little figures made up into patterns

Most people have at some time sat down idly and drawn with no real definite purpose. The result may be the kind of thing in drawing a. You simply doodle away – on schoolbooks, telephone pads or on a paper napkin. Try to draw quite unconsciously. If it is rather hard to find something straight away, here are some suggestions.

a

b. Hearts
Various hearts have been drawn here. They can be placed one on top of the other or inside one another, and decorated with lines, dots, etc.

c. Circles
These can be given rays to form suns or given petals for flowers. You can draw dots, tassels, rings inside one another of different thicknesses and many other shapes.

d. Squares
A complete chess-board of figures can be made in a square, as well as stars, striped boxes, etc.

e. Triangles
Here are some triangles in many forms. Many amusing shapes may be drawn with teeth, fringes and figures inside one another.

f. Triangles and squares
Triangles and squares offer many possibilities for creating shapes.

g. Circles and triangles
Try to combine triangles and circles to make figures, as shown in the drawing.

Arrange the figures systematically

Perhaps the finished picture now looks as it was meant to look, but it may also be too untidy. So try to arrange the individual figures more systematically.

h. In strips

The shapes can be arranged in strips to form trimmings or friezes. A trimming may perhaps be used as a hair band, guitar cord, napkin ring, watch strap or place mat. See the recorder case on page 23.

i. In rows

Take one or more figures and put them in rows beneath one another to form a complete design. This can be used for handbags, cushions, centre-pieces on tablecloths or place mats, purses, pot holders, etc. See the shoulder bag on page 23.

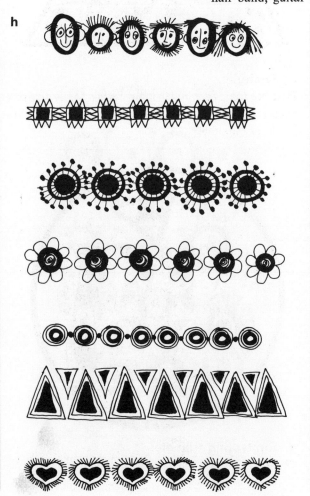

j

j. In a circle

Here the figures are set in a circle. Circle designs are suitable for table-cloths, Christmas tree rugs, purses, cushions, handbags, etc. See the finished Christmas carpet on page 48 and the felt embroidery on page 57.

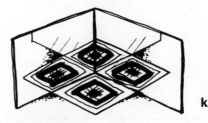

k

k. Quartered pattern

You may also place a shape in each corner of a square, or from the centre outwards, from the corners formed by two sharp folds in the material (see dotted lines).

To get a better idea of how a figure looks in quadruplicate, two mirrors can be used as shown in the drawing.

l. Shapes in panels

Divide the fabric into panels and put a different design in each. It may seem less of a task to make an embroidery this way, as you can do one small design at a time. And of course you can decide for yourself how many sections there will be.

m. Elaborate designs

A single shape can be elaborated by drawing in new outlines around and around it. The outlines can have different forms, such as dots, fringes, thick or thin lines. This type of design is suitable for pin cushions, handbags, cushions, purses, etc.

l

k

m

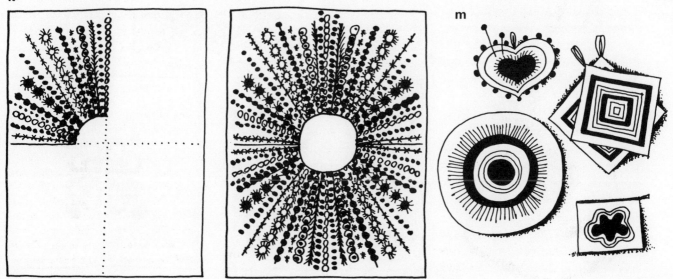

Shoulder bag

The shoulder bag, which measures 16 × 17 cm (6¼ × 7 ins) when finished, is made from natural hessian. It is embroidered with cotton yarn and chain stitch only is used.

Cut out a piece of material 44 cm (17½ ins) long, including 5 cm (2 ins) for a hem at each end, and 18 cm (7 ins) wide, including 1 cm (½ in) hem at each side.

Complete the embroidery and press it. Remember that there must first be 5 cm (2 ins) at the ends for turning in. Fold the material inside out and stitch the sides on the machine. Turn down the 5 cm (2 ins) at both ends and herring-bone stitch on the reverse. Then turn the right side outwards.

Make a twisted cord about 110 cm (44 ins) long. To see how to do this, turn to page 67. Allow an ample length of thread, as the length is reduced by the twisting. Six threads of 280 cm (112 ins) length have been used here to finish with a cord of 110 cm (44 ins) length.

The cord is sewn on along the edge of the shoulder bag and up into a sling. Start at one of the corners when sewing on the sling.

Sew on a tassel at each corner. You can make a tassel by wrapping the yarn round a strip of card, of a length equal to the required length of the tassel. Cut the threads at one end and tie them very tightly together at the other end.

Pin cushion

The pin cushion was made from hessian by a 10-year-old girl. It measures 14 × 14 cm (5½ × 5½ ins). Cut two pieces of fabric 16 × 16 cm (6 × 6 ins). Complete the embroidery and press it. Chain stitch in concentric rings has been used, with wool remnants in different shades of blue, yellow and green.

Place the right sides of both pieces of material together and stitch three of the sides on the machine. Turn out the right side and stuff with kapok or other filling. The final side is then sewn together by hand with small stitches.

Recorder case

The case for the recorder is very easy to make. It is made in the same manner as the etui with the cord embroidery on page 86, but the pocket is made much longer to suit the length of the recorder. The lining may be left out. Hessian is also used here, 76 × 7 cm (30 × 3 ins) for a small recorder, and the embroidery is worked with cotton. Chain stitch in rings is used. A carrier of twisted yarn is provided at the top. Look at the chapter on Cords to see how this is made.

You can see from the completed items on the right and the drawings on the left how a single shape can be employed. On the shoulder bag, rounded squares with circles in the centre have been set in rows to form a complete pattern. The size and colour of the circles are varied to give the embroidery more life. On the recorder case, circles have been set along a line. The pin cushion is made by continuing to work concentric rings.

Mirror pictures

The clown
This is embroidered with linen yarn on linen. Satin stitch and stem stitch were used.

Butterflies
The butterflies were embroidered with cotton yarn on linen, using back stitch, buttonhole stitch wheels, buttonhole stitch (around the wheels), stem stitch, chain stitch and French knots. The butterflies can be used for place mats, on boxes, for bookcovers, pin cushions, etc.

a and b. Fold a piece of smooth paper at the centre and unfold it again. Paint any kind of shape on one side of the fold with water colour and a soft brush. It may only be a blob of colour dropped from the brush and nothing more.

c. Fold the paper again before the paint is dry and press it together hard so that the paint comes off on the opposite side.

d. Unfold the paper and look at the shape that has now been formed. Perhaps it is good enough as it is, or it may form the basis for a more exciting shape.

The girl
Anne Marie was aged 11 when she embroidered the girl with the blond hair. She had made a mirror picture on which she continued to draw. When the drawing was later traced onto fine linen she started embroidering with embroidery cotton in various colours.

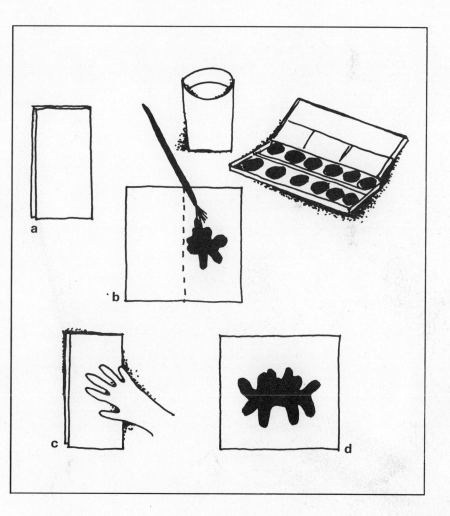

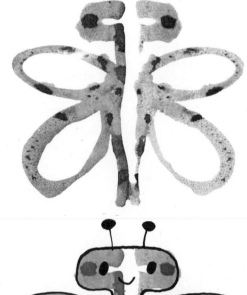

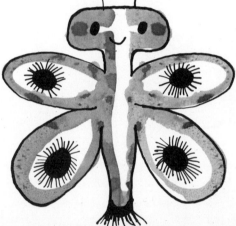

For embroidery use, shapes must be absolutely distinct. You must therefore draw them in clearly with, for example, a pencil.

You may, perhaps, see several different shapes in the same blobs, as shown in drawing b.

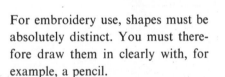

a. Here you can see how a butterfly came into existence. First the paint impression was made and then the outlines were drawn and decorated with a design in each wing. Finally it was traced on to fabric and embroidered. See the examples in colour on page 24.

b. The blobs at the top can suggest various figures. Here they have become a troll (a rather hairy creature in Scandinavian mythology) and a cow.

c. These figures are a little more complicated, and it was necessary to paint and press a few times to get everything in.

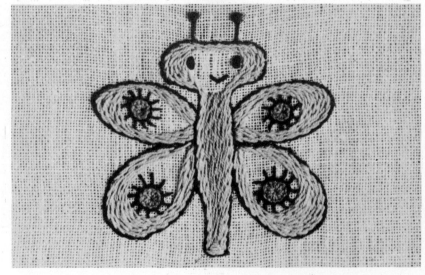

a

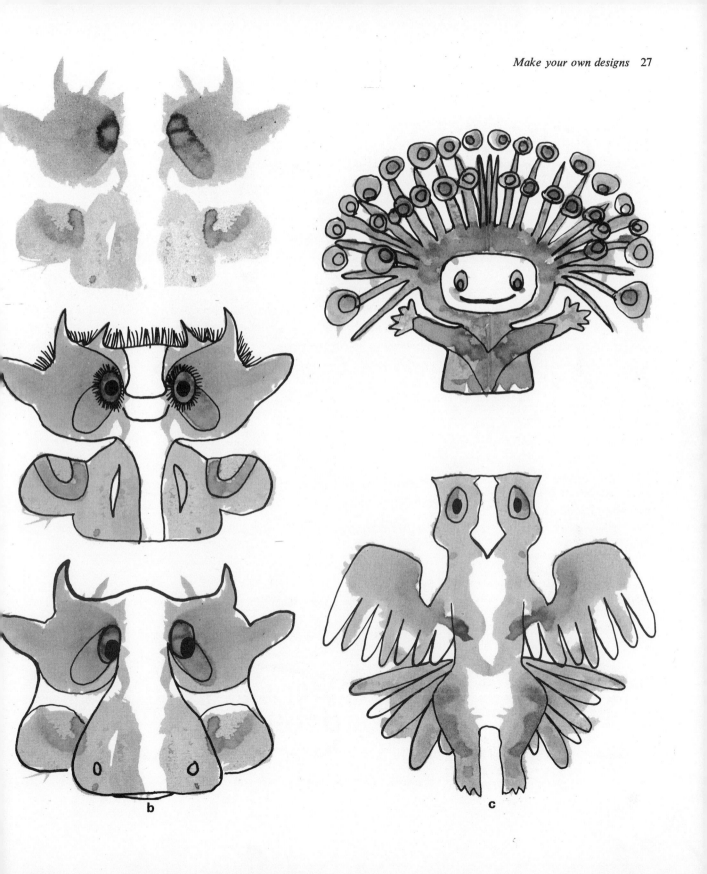

b

c

DIFFERENT STITCHES

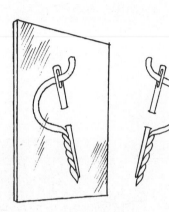

The stitches in this book have been drawn and described for right-handed people, but if you are left-handed, you can see the stitches the other way round by using a mirror. This makes it easier to follow the drawings.

For beginners, young and old

It is easiest to embroider on coarse fabrics using a large needle with a blunt point. Embroider with thick yarn or with several threads in the needle. The work will then progress quickly.

Suitable fabrics include floorcloths, hessian and jute aida; see the examples on page 7.

On the next ten pages we show embroideries, some of which were made by children. The others are so simple to follow that children can easily tackle them.

Embroidery on cardboard

Make a drawing on a piece of cardboard, for example on the back of a writing pad. Colour the drawing, and then prick holes at even intervals, using a thick needle through the lines to be embroidered. Then sew up and down using running stitch so that every other interval is covered. Finally, fill in the intervals. See how to make running stitches on page 30.

You can see from the three illustrations how cardboard embroidery looks. The little house was drawn and embroidered by Anders, who is 5 years old, the clown by 7-year-old Johan, and the Red Indian picture by 10-year-old Pernille.

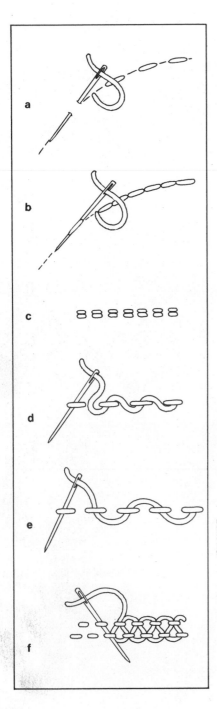

Running stitch (tacking stitch)

a. Running stitch is sewn from the top downwards or from right to left, using stitches and intervals of equal size.

Double running stitch

b. For double running stitch, one row of running stitches is made first. Then you work backwards – also using running stitch – so that the intervals are covered.

c. Small, close running stitch in two rows will look like dots.

d, e and f. You can sew with a different thread, perhaps in another colour, through one or more rows of running stitch.

A woollen bird decorated with buttons

The bird embroidery is sewn directly onto the fabric without first tracing the design. Wool is used, together with raffia and buttons, but there is nothing to stop you from using anything available in the way of snap fasteners, hooks, hair pins, matches, sticks, etc. In that case of course the picture cannot be washed.

Stitches: For the bird embroidery we have used stem stitch, chain stitch, buttonhole stitch (around the buttons on the bird's body) and couching (the raffia for the tail).

In some places, the embroidery is in double yarn (the stems of the flowers). Small tufts of raffia have been sewn onto the head.

Embroidery on floorcloths

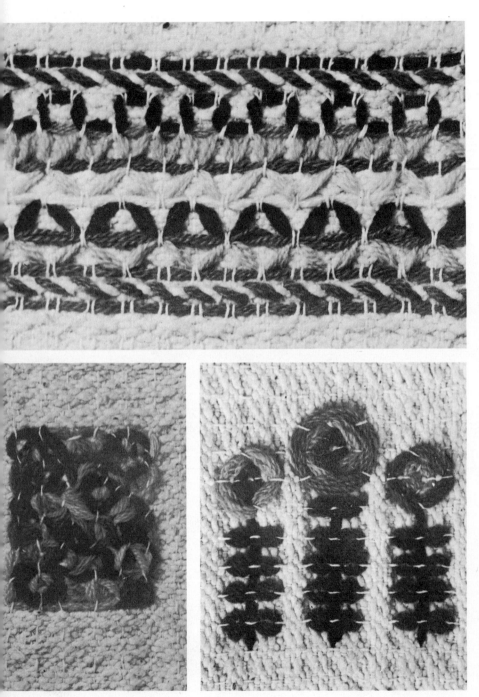

Floorcloths and dishcloths are cheap and easy to use for embroidery. There are small loops on both sides of the material through which you can pull threads.
Look at our suggestions.

1. Fill the whole floorcloth with bands in different colours and then use it for a small cushion, or a place mat.

2. Make an abstract pattern by pulling different-coloured threads in and out among each other.

3. Here flowers have been embroidered. Several rows close together or opposite one another form a good design for a cushion.

4. The girl with the stylish head decoration is worked from a child's drawing. Try to make your own designs or get ideas from other pages in this book.

Cross stitch and Holbein (or double running) stitch

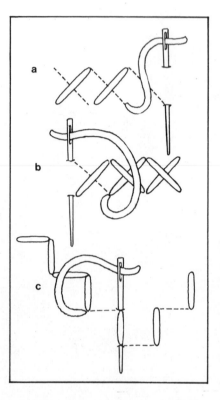

Materials:

Many materials are suitable for cross stitch embroidery, particularly aida fabrics; these are available in fine and coarse qualities. The coarsest, used for the steamer on the right, is called jute aida. The little train is embroidered on one of the finer aidas, called pearl aida. Other materials are canvas, and evenweave linen, where we embroider across counted threads; see the fish and the elephant. See also fabric examples on page 7.

Try to draw your own designs in a squared exercise book. The squares can perhaps be coloured with a felt-tip pen or paint. You can design borders, patterns, houses, men, women, etc.

Cross stitch

Cross stitch consists of an under-and-over stitch.

a. Start by sewing the under-stitches from left to right.

b. The over-stitches are then sewn in reverse, i.e. from right to left.

It is important that all over-stitches should be in the same direction.

Holbein (or double running) stitch

c. Start by sewing the stitches from right to left. On the way back, fill in the intervals.

The fish and the elephant are sewn with wool on coarse linen. Note the difference between the two ways of using cross stitch. The background to the fish is completely filled in, the fish being left entirely white. All its outlines are embroidered in Holbein stitch. This type of cross stitch is also called Assisi embroidery. The elephant has no background but is itself filled in with stitches except the ear.

The steamer is worked in wool on jute aida. The stitches used are cross stitch, double running stitch (at the top) and Holbein stitch (around the sun). For double running stitch, see page 30.

The train is embroidered with cotton yarn on pearl aida.

Rya work

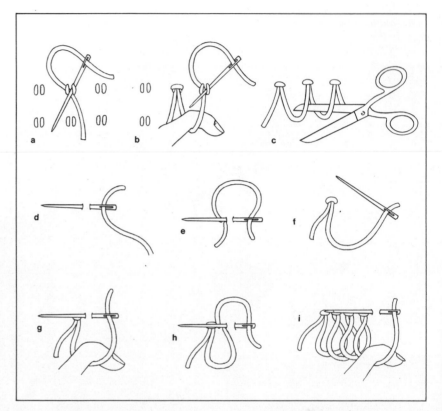

Rya is easier than you may think, particularly if fairly coarse materials are used. Apart from the fabric and yarn specially designed for Rya work, many other fabrics may be used – such as canvas and aida. Work with a large needle with a blunt point.

It is not necessary to place Rya stitches in a straight line. You will see on pages 64 – 65 how Rya work can be used in different ways; as loops of fishing line around the flower head or as a delightful lion's mane made of string. See also the fish in the photograph.

Drawings a, b and c show traditional Rya work on a specially woven base: small loops arranged in pairs. If several rows are to be worked, you start from the bottom left corner and work towards the right.

a. Using one or more threads in the needle, lead it from right to left up into the left loop and then from right to left down through the right loop. Pull the thread so that a kind of knot is formed.

b. Do the same with the next two loops and hold down the thread between the loops in a bow with your finger. If you want uniform bows, use a ruler instead of your finger.

c. The bows can stay as they are or be cut open as shown.

Drawings d, e, f, g, h and i show how Rya is worked in other fabrics.

d. Sew a horizontal stitch from right to left under a couple of threads.

e. and f. With the thread at the top, sew one more horizontal stitch under a couple of threads and pull the thread so that a knot is formed.

g. Make one more stitch and hold down the loop with the finger.

h. Sew the next stitch with the thread lying at the top and pull the stitch to form a knot.

i. Carry on in this way.
The loops made can either stay as they are or be cut open.

In the little flower, the Rya loops are worked into a ring with fishing line on hessian. See also page 64. Bottom left: the Rya fabric has rows of regular holes and is therefore suitable for beginners to practise different stitches. The fabric is itself attractive, and if different colours are chosen for the stitches, the work can be really beautiful to look at.

Stitches: running stitch, chain stitch, back stitch, satin stitch, stem stitch, herring-bone stitch, cross stitch and Rya work.

The fish is worked on Rya fabric with embroidery wool. The outline is a crocheted cord (see page 66). The head of the big fish is worked across the stripes in the weave, and rows of Rya work have been sewn on the body.

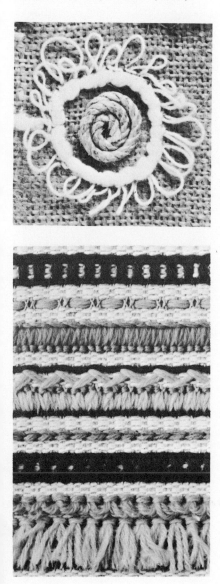

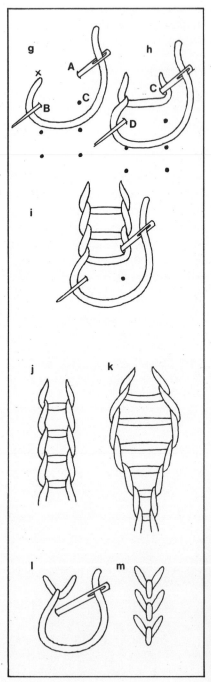

In this little embroidery, Karina has practised chain stitch. The embroidery is linen yarn on felt.

Chain stitch

a. Chain stitch is worked from above downwards. Lay the thread on the left and hold it with the left thumb. Push in the needle where it last came up and bring it up a little farther along.

Chain stitch in a circle

b. Start at x and end as shown in the drawing.

Detached chain stitches (millefleurs)

c. Push the needle through from the top and hold the thread down with the left thumb. Push it in where it last came up and make a stitch.

d. Fasten the loop with a small stitch at the bottom.

e. The finished stitch.

f. This shows how a flower can be worked.

Open chain stitch

Open chain stitch can be worked irregularly to create shapes as in drawings j and k, or along two parallel lines as in drawing i.

g. Push the needle up at x and hold the thread with the left thumb. Push in at A and up again at B. The loop should be pulled only lightly.

h. Now push the needle into the fabric at C, with the thread from the last stitch under the needle, and up again at D.

i. Continue in this way and fasten off the last loop with a small stitch either side.

j. This shows a row of narrow stitches.

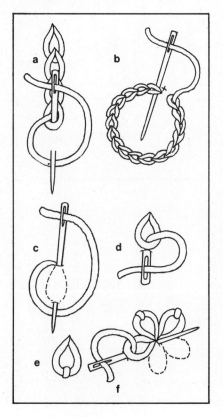

k. Amusing shapes can be made if the stitches are worked at irregular widths.

Fly stitch

l and m. Fly stitches are open chain stitches. They are worked as shown in the drawing.

Stem stitch

n. Stem stitches are worked from below and up. Push the needle up into the fabric and insert it farther along the line, bringing it out again half-way back between the second and first holes. Continue in this way, bringing the needle out of the same

The princess was embroidered by an 11-year-old girl. The lace of the dress is worked in detached chain stitch. The decoration on the dress is worked in chain stitch in circles with beads sewn into the centres. Flowers are worked between these circles in detached chain stitch (millefleurs). The rest is worked in stem stitch.

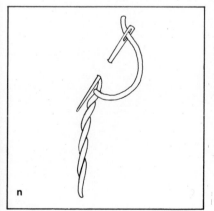

n

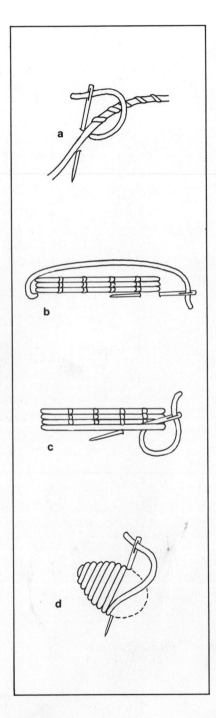

a

b

c

d

hole as you used in the previous stitch. Take the same amount of fabric onto the needle every time and always lay the thread on the same side.

Couching

Couching is used for working outlines (see the owl on page 42) or for filling in areas (see the picture of the tiger).

a. Place one or more threads along the line you wish to work and secure with another, perhaps finer, thread.
Stitch the ends to the reverse and fasten.
The circles in the flower, bottom right, and the snail's shell on the left are worked in this way.

b and c. This shows couching with a single thread.
Push the needle up to the left, take the thread right across the shape and sew it down on the way back with small stitches into the fabric at regular intervals.
The tiger with her cub is worked in this way.

Satin stitch

Satin stitch is used for covering a surface.

d. Sew right across the shape, pushing the needle down and up again just outside the tracing so that this is covered.

It is difficult to make round shapes neatly with this stitch.
It is easiest to work checks and square shapes as in the clown's hat on page 24, where you follow the threads in the fabric.

The tiger with her cub is worked in couching as in Figs. b and c. Outlines and cheeks are worked in stem stitch. Eyes, nose and other places on the tail and face are filled in with satin stitch.
The sun is worked in couching, as in Fig. a, and the petals in back stitch. The embroidery is on hessian using embroidery wool. See mounting on page 87 (wall hangings).
The snail is worked in stem stitch and its shell in couching, as in Fig. a. The horns are French knots. It is worked on hessian using embroidery wool. See mounting on page 81 (box with embroidery).
The flower embroidery is also worked on hessian with embroidery wool. The two outer golden rings are in couching as in Fig. a. The petals are detached chain stitch (millefleurs). The green leaves are filled in with satin stitch, and the rest is worked in stem stitch. See mounting on page 83 (spectacles case).

The owl is worked on hessian using embroidery wool. It is worked in French knots, tight herring-bone stitch (the wing), chain stitch, stem stitch and couching (outlines and feet). Pattern, page 112.

The tree with the birds was worked by a 12-year-old girl. Linen yarn was used on cotton fabric. The trunk was worked in chain stitch, the branches in two rows of buttonhole stitch (facing one another), and the birds in stem stitch. The birds' eyes are buttonhole stitch wheels, later provided with a little eye in the centre. Pattern, page 110.

The little bird with the apple is worked entirely in back stitch. It is wool on hessian. Pattern, page 108.

The fish is worked by pulling threads through the fabric. The eye is in stem stitch. Embroidery wool on hessian has been used. Pattern, page 108.

Back stitch

a. X shows where to start. Work the stitches from the top downwards. Push the needle up through the fabric, make a stitch backwards and push the needle up a little in front of the first stitch and at the same length. Push down again where the needle came up the first time and then up forward again.

French knot

b. Push the needle up where the knot is to be. Hold the thread with the left thumb and lead the needle under the thread.

c and d. Turn the needle across the thread and push in directly behind the point where it came up. Bring it out where the next knot is to be.

e. The finished knot.

Bullion knot

f and g. You can also make bullion knots. Make a back stitch of the length you wish the knot to be and bring the needle up where the thread is. Twist the thread around the needle as many times as is suitable for the length of the back stitch. Hold the twisted thread with the left thumb and pull the needle through. Finally, push the needle through again at the point where it first went in.

h. These bullion knots can be worked into a flower. In this case, push the needle up in the centre and work the knots from there.

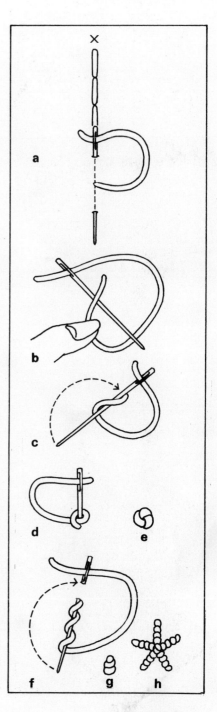

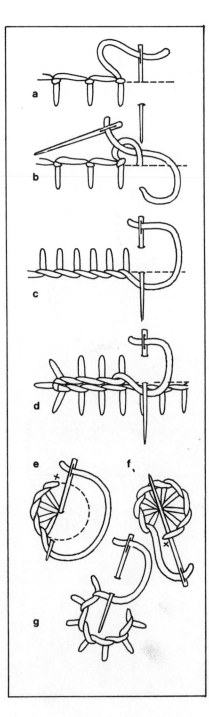

Blanket stitch

Blanket stitch is a simple buttonhole stitch, and is worked from left to right. The stitch is worked in two stages.

a. First work a stitch into the fabric.
b. Then lead the needle behind and through the loop formed. Pull the stitch.

Blanket stitch can also be used for finishing an edge. See page 91.

Buttonhole stitch

c. Buttonhole stitch is worked from left to right. Make a stitch with the thread behind the needle and pull the stitch straight down.

Buttonhole stitch in double rows

d. First work one row of buttonhole stitches. Turn with a few stitches and continue back – again using buttonhole stitch.

Buttonhole stitch wheels

e. X shows where to start. Push the needle in at the centre of the circle and up again just outside the tracing.
f. Finish the wheel by pushing the needle under the first stitch and down through the centre.

A different version of buttonhole stitch

g. Here the buttonhole stitch is worked out from the centre to form rays.

Vandyke stitch

h. Bring the needle up at A and work a small stitch at B.

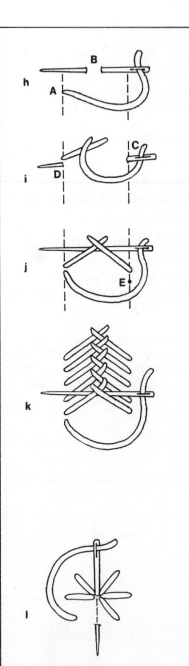

i. Push the needle in at C to form a cross and come up at D.

j. Lead the needle under the cross without going into the fabric and push the needle in at E.

k. Continue in this way. Do not pull the stitches too tight.

Stars

l. Stars are worked as shown in the drawing. Always work outwards from the centre.

Herring-bone stitch

Herring-bone stitch is worked from below upwards. It can be worked with large intervals or closely, as desired.

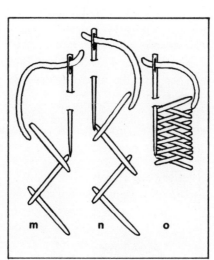

It may be used as a decorative stitch or worked across a hem as shown on page 90. Work alternately on the right and left sides and take care that the thread is always lying on the correct side.

m. The thread must be kept on the left, and the sewing is worked on the right side.

n. The reverse of m.

o. This shows a row of close herring-bone stitches.

The trees are worked in linen yarn on linen. Pattern and description of stitches on page 95.

APPLIQUÉ

Gluing on

There are many ways of making appliqué – from the very easy to the very complicated. We shall start with the easy way which needs no sewing. What we use here are old rags, yarn remnants, scissors and adhesive. In fact, all manner of things can be used if the work need not be washable. For example, we have worked here with a stick and the plastic netting used for packaging fruit. Raffia, matches etc. can also be used. You will need a soft board to hang the appliqué work on.

Felt appliqué is an easy method of appliqué work. Felt does not fray and is easy to glue on to other materials. See pages 54 – 57.

The appliqué picture

This big appliqué picture was made by Susanne, Birgitte and Anders. They sat around a table with a large pile of rags and yarn remnants in the middle, and each of them cut out lots of small shapes. Shapes and yarn were glued on.

As the cuttings were finished they were fixed with pins on to a piece of soft board. It developed into a big gay tapestry for hanging anywhere in their room where a little brightness was needed.

Appliqué, sewn on and ironed on

Useful hints

When making appliqué, it is advisable to choose designs that are as simple as possible. Shapes with lots of corners and edges are difficult to sew on neatly. And if you want to be absolutely sure of a good result it is wise to use thin white iron-on Vilene on the back of the 'rags'. This will stop the fabric from fraying easily and it is much easier to handle. When the separate parts are cut, sew them onto the piece of fabric chosen to form the background.

If you want to avoid sewing altogether, you can do this by using Bondaweb. Iron it onto the back of the 'rag', cut out, remove the piece of paper on one side of the Bondaweb and then iron the rag onto the fabric.

The Christmas carpet

A job as big as the Christmas carpet is best done by several people. Three worked on this: Lars, aged 8; Pia, aged 11; and Anne Marie, aged 13. Patterns for the figures are on pages 116 – 121.
Materials:
Linen, 140 × 140 cm (56 × 56 ins).
Fabric remnants in various colours.
Iron-on Vilene.
Yarn in various colours.
a. The children first folded the fabric into four (the dotted lines). They then measured 45 cm (18 ins) from the centre towards all four sides and marked out a circle of that radius with pins. They then tacked the whole circumference of the circle and removed the pins.
b. Vilene was ironed onto a large number of attractively coloured fabric pieces. With the Vilene on the back, the fabric was not so inclined to fray and was easy to cut out.
c. They then started to cut out pixies, Christmas trees, stars, etc. They drew the shapes with pencil on the back of the fabric before they cut them out. They therefore had to remember that they would face the other way when the fabric was turned right side up.
As the shapes were cut out they were laid on the linen. They experimented a little to find out what looked best. When they had enough shapes they fixed them with pins and then tacked them onto the linen. The different parts were now sewn on. This meant a lot of work, and they took it in turns to sew. Various stitches were used for sewing on the shapes: buttonhole stitch, hemming stitch, herring-bone stitch and alternate large and small stitches as shown in the drawing on page 51.
Finally eyes, mouths, horse's tail, etc. were embroidered.
A Christmas carpet may be used as a tablecloth at Christmas-time or placed under the Christmas tree.

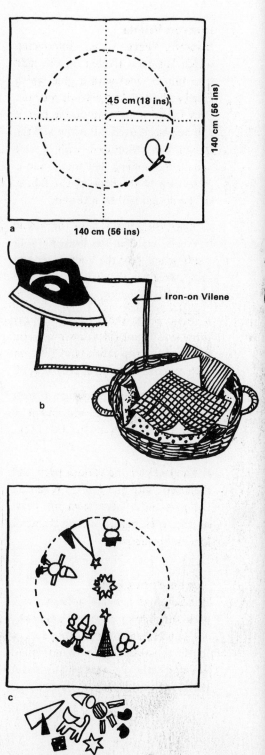

a 140 cm (56 ins) 45 cm (18 ins) 140 cm (56 ins)

Iron-on Vilene

b

c

Iron-on Vilene

Iron-on Vilene is an interfacing which has been treated on one side (the shinier side) with a glue which fuses with the fabric when ironed on. This fabric is so transparent that it can be placed over a drawing and the design can be traced with a soft pencil. Remember that the Vilene is ironed on to the back of the fabric, so the design will be reversed.

a. Place the shiny side of the Vilene upwards, transfer the drawing with a soft pencil, turn the Vilene over and draw the lines through on this side also.

b. Now place the Vilene with the shiny side (glued side) downwards on the back of the fabric and iron on with a warm iron; setting: silk/wool.

c and d. Cut out the design, turn it around to the fabric side and it is ready to be sewn on to the background fabric.

e. First tack on the various parts and then sew onto the fabric. When all the parts have been sewn on, draw or trace eyes, mouth, etc. on the work and embroider.

Vilene Bondaweb

Bondaweb is a nylon adhesive web with supporting paper on one side, and can be used to glue two pieces of fabric together. It can stand up to washing and dry-cleaning without the glued sections coming apart.

a Iron-on Vilene with shiny side up

← Drawing

← Material

b Iron-on Vilene with matt side up

c

d

e

Draw a design on the paper side of the Bondaweb. Then place this with the adhesive side against the reverse of the fabric and press it on the paper side with an iron. Allow to cool. Cut out the shape and slowly pull off the supporting paper. Place the section on the background fabric with the adhesive side (where the paper was removed) facing downwards. Press hard using a steam iron, or an ordinary iron and a damp pressing rag, and the section will be firmly in place.

The bee and the ladybird

This picture was made in a way slightly more difficult than the others.

f. Cut out a piece of iron-on Vilene to the desired shape. Place the Vilene on the fabric and iron on with a warm iron.

g. Cut out the figure, allowing for a hem of about $\frac{1}{2}$ cm ($\frac{1}{4}$ in.). Clip the hem in the curved places.

h. Turn over the hem and tack along the edge.

i. Place the figure on the fabric, tack on and then sew on firmly with very small stitches.
Then decorate with embroidery.
Patterns for the bee and ladybird are on pages 94 and 95.

Stitches: stem stitch (the heads), chain stitch (stripes), back stitch (wings), buttonhole stitch wheels and French knots.

Various stitches for sewing on shapes

Appliqué cut-outs can be sewn onto the background with many different stitches, such as:

j. Hemming stitch

k. Buttonhole stitch

l. Herring-bone stitch

m. By sewing machine using zig-zag stitch. See the pirate on page 53.

n. A stitch you invent yourself. For example, trees, birds and other animals can be sewn on with alternate small and large stitches to look like feathers or hair bristling out in all directions. See the Christmas carpet on page 48.

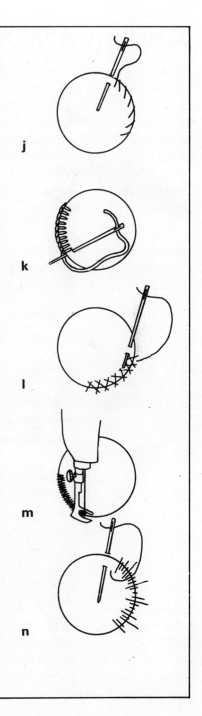

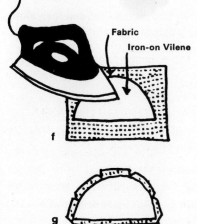

Appliqué work, sewn on by machine

This form of appliqué work is good practice in using a sewing machine. But it also means that you *must* have a machine equipped for zig-zag sewing. Set the machine at a suitable stitch length and width and work to and fro. You can in fact embroider with a sewing machine and produce many amusing effects.

Pirate

The pirate is worked from the drawing on the left, which was drawn by an 8-year-old boy.

He drew the pirate's various parts on iron-on Vilene, ironed these onto the coloured fabric and cut them out (see drawings a, b, c and d on page 50). At the places where the pieces overlap (such as the arms, which extend a little beneath the body) he allowed a little extra fabric. For the cloak he cut out a complete circle.

The round cloak was then tacked and sewn onto the background fabric on the machine, using zig-zag stitching, and then decorated with a few zig-zag borders.

All the other pieces were then tacked onto the fabric and finally zig-zagged on using the sewing machine. He changed the stitch width and length several times and also changed the colour of the thread.

Hair and beard were worked by sewing to and fro several times.

The black felt buttons were glued on.

FELT

Pernille. V. J.

Felt is a wonderful material to work with. It does not fray and it is available in many different colours. But make sure you buy good quality felt as it is easier to work with and lasts longer.

Felt can be used for very many things: appliqué, matchbox decoration, handbags, purses, pot holders, soft toys, dolls, etc.

Felt, glued on

The easiest way to work with felt is simply to glue the cut-out pieces to the background.

Take care not to apply so much glue that it soaks through the material and stains the right side.

Felt, sewn on

As the surface of felt is a little 'dead', embroidery will greatly improve it. You can also mix the work a little; embroider in some places and glue in others.

But there should be no glue under the places to be embroidered as the needle will jam and come out sticky.

Horse

The long-legged horse is worked from the drawing on the left. Notice the little changes that often have to be made when a drawing is transformed into an embroidery.

The various pieces for the horse are embroidered on with open chain stitch (after tacking on). Green dots have been worked on the blue surface so that it does not look too large and bare.

You can also avoid the job of embroidering on the pieces and be content with gluing them on or ironing them on with Bondaweb.

Felt dolls

All the felt figures except the little cat are made from the same basic shape – only colour, face, ears and feet are different. These dolls have been made to demonstrate the many possibilities there are in a single design. Not much variation was needed for it to become an entirely different figure.

Working instructions: The patterns are on page 100. Body and head are in one piece, but the different heads are drawn beside the basic shape to show the variations. Draw the pieces on transparent paper and trace them onto the felt. Front and rear are the same. No need to allow for hems. It is easiest to embroider the faces before the pieces are cut out.

Place the front and back against one another, wrong sides together, and sew them together with small over-sewing stitches, using sewing silk of the same colour as the felt. But leave an opening at the top of the head and at the side. Using little tacking stitches or the machine, work along the

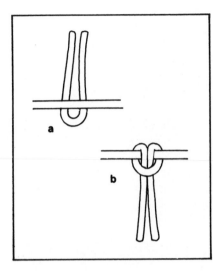

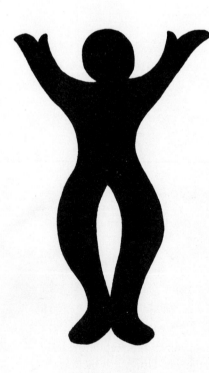

dotted lines at the neck and ears. This separates the head from the body and makes it more flexible. The ears are separated from the head in the same way. Push cotton wool, kapok or other stuffing through the two openings. Use a pencil to help until arms and legs are firmly stuffed. Use oversewing stitch to close the openings.

Tails can be oversewn together, stuffed and sewn on the back of the body.

Boots and hat are cut as shown in the pattern, oversewn together and glued to the doll.

Finally, the dolls are given hair. Bits of yarn are cut and sewn together in small bundles, using back stitch; see page 61.

The pompons for the clown on page 54 are made as shown on page 58. The Hawaiian girl's skirt is made from a pipe cleaner and a few raffia ends about 10 cm (4 ins) long. Each piece of raffia is glued to the pipe cleaner, and the two ends are pulled through the loop as shown in drawings a and b. The ends of the raffia are then cut to a length of about 2 cm ($\frac{3}{4}$ in.). The yellow dress is cut as shown in the pattern on page 100. Front and back are the same, but the front is folded double and $\frac{1}{2}$ cm ($\frac{1}{4}$ in.) is allowed at the back for an overlap. Allow for a hem on the shoulders and side seams. Finally, snap fasteners are sewn on at the back.

The dancer

The dancer at the bottom left is cut from black felt folded double. Other symmetrical figures can be cut in the same way; see page 25. The figure is glued to a felt background.

Circular design ▶

This was done by gluing, embroidery and sewing on beads. The pattern is on page 98. The large circle of orange felt was sewn on a dark brown background with open chain stitch.

Seven smaller circles in a lighter orange were glued on in a circle. Buttonhole stitches in dark brown were embroidered around these.

Finally, a circle of pink felt and a brown bead were sewn into the centre of each circle.

Fireplace glove ▶

A black sweep was glued onto one side of the orange glove. Pattern on page 125 and sewing instructions on page 83.

Decorated boxes ▶

Seven-year-old Johan made these boxes. Spread newspapers on a table. Place some boxes (matchboxes, cigar boxes, etc.) in one pile, the felt pieces in another. Add scissors and glue, and work can begin.

Glue the felt directly onto the box to cover it. Then glue the cut-out shapes on top.

POMPONS

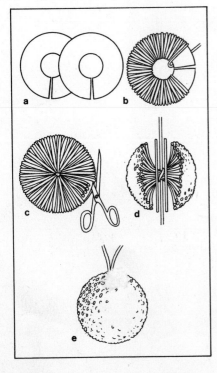

Pompons are not very difficult to make. They are generally used for attaching to the ends of tying cords on baby clothes or for the tops of caps. You can also make small soft animals by joining several pompons. They can be made of different colours and cut into shape. Eyes, beaks, claws, etc. can be cut from felt and glued on. Pipe cleaners can also be used for claws; see the parrot.

Instructions

a. Cut out two cardboard rings (with a cut and a hole in the centre) in the size you wish the pompon to be.

b. Place the cardboard rings together and wind yarn around them as closely and evenly as possible.

c. When the hole is completely filled, cut along the edge between the cardboard pieces.

d. Tie a string, preferably double, around all the threads between the cardboard pieces, pull tightly and remove the cardboard pieces.

e. Trim the pompon so that it becomes round and neat; then steam it over a kettle of boiling water, taking care not to scald yourself. The ends of the string are used for tying or sewing the pompon on.

The owls

Two pompons are needed for an owl. They are tied together with the ends of the string. Tie several knots so that they are securely joined and cut off the ends. Cut the eyes and beaks from felt or strong paper and glue on.

The rabbits

The rabbits are made like the owls by tying two pompons together. Make another, very small pompon for the tail and glue it on. Cut the ears and eyes from white felt. Here the ears are double and joined together by oversewing stitch. Paint on the black of the eyes with a felt-tip pen. Cut the teeth from white paper and glue the pieces on.

The lion

For the lion's head, make a pompon with the inner layer of yarn of a darker yellow than the outer layer. When winding of the pompon is finished and it is cut open, cut the light yellow face section quite short, leaving the dark yellow section as it is and with the rest of the long ends looking like a mane. Before the eyes and nose are put on, it looks like a flower. Make a small orange pompon for the nose and, together with the black felt eyes, glue in place.

Make a dark yellow pompon for the body. This is tied together with the head. Make the tail from a crocheted cord (see page 66) with a tuft at the end and sew it on.

The parrot

This is made from a large and a small pompon. First carry out the winding with white yarn and then with dark lilac, light lilac, purple and finally white again. When the pompon is cut open you will have amusing stripes. Tie the pompons together securely and cut off the ends. Beak and eyes are felt. The beak is doubled over and joined by oversewing stitch, except for the side towards the face. Push in cotton wool or other stuffing and glue beak and eyes in place. Glue a tuft of yarn in different colours to the back to form a tail. The claws are made from pipe cleaners wound with yarn and sewn or glued on.

DOLLS AND DOLLS' CLOTHES

The little doll with the fat tummy is made from white towelling. Cotton jersey or other cotton fabrics may also be used. The doll is about 37 cm (14½ ins) long.

Cutting

From pages 102 – 105, trace the pattern pieces, which have no seam allowance, on transparent paper and lay them on the fabric. Cut two pieces of all the patterns, except for the bib and the hood, allowing ½ cm (¼ in) for the seams.

The head

First embroider the face, using thin embroidery cotton. Then lay the pieces for the face right side to right side. Stitch them together except at the top where a section must be left open for the stuffing. Trim the seams and turn the right side out. Stitch from the right side along the dotted lines for the ears. Stuff with kapok, foam rubber or other stuffing and close the hole at the top by oversewing.

The hair

Cut pieces of wool about 15 cm (6 ins) long for the hair. Sew them to the head in small bundles with backstitch as shown here.

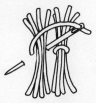

The body

Lay the pieces for the tummy right sides together, and stitch the centre seam. Press the seam. Then place front and back pieces against one another, right side to right side, and stitch all the way round except for the neck. Trim the hems and turn the right side out. Push the stuffing in

through the neck opening. Use a pencil to ensure that legs and arms are firmly stuffed. The tummy must also be firmly stuffed, but where arms and legs join the body the stuffing should not be too hard. It is better for the doll to be a little flexible here so that it can bend its arms and legs. Sew up the neck and finally sew the head to the body.

Dolls' clothes

A few basic designs for dolls' clothes are shown here. From these you can make a great variety of clothes for the dolls.

The patterns

The patterns for the dolls' clothes are on pages 103 – 105 but no allowance has been made for seams. Trace the pieces on transparent paper and cut them out.

LILAC-COLOURED DRESS WITH TROUSERS
Cutting

Place the pattern pieces on the fabric. Front and back of the dress are the same, except that the front must be folded double and 1 cm (½ in) hem must be allowed in the centre of the back for the seam. Allow a hem of

$\frac{1}{2}$ cm ($\frac{1}{4}$ in) for sleeve openings, and for shoulder and side seams, and 1 cm ($\frac{1}{2}$ in) at the bottom. But no hem is needed at the neck because of the edging.

Fold the trousers along the line between the legs. Allow 1 cm ($\frac{1}{2}$ in) at the top for the hem and $\frac{1}{2}$ cm ($\frac{1}{4}$ in) at the sides. No hem allowance is needed at the trouser legs because of the edging.

The dress

Place front and back pieces right sides together, and stitch the shoulder seams. Press the seams apart. Turn the hem allowances on the back pieces to the reverse and work herring-bone stitch along them. Then edge neck and sleeve openings with bias binding, perhaps in a different colour from the dress. (Bias binding, see page 91.) Allow a little of the bias binding to extend sufficiently at both sides of the neck at the back to make tying ribbons.

Trim the seams and, at the sleeve openings, turn the bias binding right over onto the reverse so that it cannot be seen and join with small herring-bone stitch. An edge of the bias binding must be visible at the neck. Taper off the two ends of the tying ribbons by using small oversewing stitches. Sew the side seams together and press. Take up the dress at the bottom and work herring-bone stitch along the hem. Neaten the seams with overcasting stitch to prevent the fabric from fraying.

The trousers

First edge the trouser legs with bias binding. Then stitch the side seams and press. Make a hem at the waist and stitch it, leaving room for elastic to be threaded through. Neaten the seams with overcasting stitch and pull the elastic through.

ORANGE DRESS WITH HOOD
Cutting

Place the pattern pieces on the fabric. Front and back pieces for the dress are the same but the front is folded double, and 1 cm ($\frac{1}{2}$ in) is allowed in the centre of the back for the seam. Allow about 1 cm ($\frac{1}{2}$ in) for a hem on the sleeves and at the bottom edge, $\frac{1}{2}$ cm ($\frac{1}{4}$ in) on shoulder and side seams. You need no allowance for a hem at the neck because of the edging. Allow $\frac{1}{2}$ cm ($\frac{1}{4}$ in) for seams for the pockets, the back edge of the brim and the crown of the hood. No allowance for a seam is necessary at the hood's bottom and front edges.

The dress

Place the front and back with the right sides together and stitch shoulder and side seams. Press the seams. Cut a few notches under the arms so that the seams do not pull when the right side is turned out.

Tack the seams on the pockets to the reverse and work herring-bone stitch along the seam at the top. First tack on the pockets and then sew them onto the dress using small stitches. On the back section, turn the seams in at the centre onto the reverse side and work herring-bone stitch along them. Turn up the dress at the bottom and on the sleeves. Work herring-bone stitch along the hems.

The neck may be edged with bias binding (see page 91). Allow enough of the bias binding to extend at both ends of the neck to form tying ribbons. Work the ends into narrow tying ribbons with small stitches. Neaten the seams with overcasting stitch.

The doll pattern can be used for many other things, such as a Teddy bear, a lion, a troll or a cat. It is easy to alter the face and the ears and to sew on a tail.

The hood
With the right sides facing one another, sew the brim and crown sections together. First edge the bottom of the hood with bias binding, and then the brim. Allow the bias strip to extend at both sides so that there are two ends for tying. Work the ends into narrow ribbons with small stitches. Neaten the seam with overcasting stitch.

DUNGAREES WITH FLAP
Cutting
Place the pattern pieces on the fabric. Allow 1 cm ($\frac{1}{2}$ in) for hem at the bottom of the trouser legs, $\frac{1}{2}$ cm ($\frac{1}{4}$ in) at the centre front and back and between the legs; no allowance for hems at other places because of the edging.

Sewing
Place the pieces right sides together and stitch the seams at front and back centres. Press. Then place the trousers right sides together so that the seams at the centre front and centre back meet between the legs. Stitch the seams between the legs. Press. Turn up the trouser legs. Work herringbone stitch along the seams.
Edge with bias binding around the back and up the flap. Sew a pair of narrow strips of bias binding for tying on to the flap.

BIB
Cut out the bib from, for example, towelling, following the pattern on page 104. First edge the bib itself with bias binding, and then the neck. Leave the ends of the bias binding extending at both sides to form tying ribbons. Work the ends into narrow ribbons using small stitches.

NIGHT-DRESS
Cutting
Place the pattern pieces on the fabric. Front and back pieces are the same, but the back is folded double and 1 cm ($\frac{1}{2}$ in) is added to the front pieces at the centre. No allowance is made for a seam at the neck and sleeve openings because of the edging. Allow $\frac{1}{2}$ cm ($\frac{1}{4}$ in) at the sides, on the shoulders and at the bottom. Cut out a long piece $62 \times 5\frac{1}{2}$ cm ($24\frac{1}{2} \times 2$ ins) for the frill.

Sewing
Place the front pieces against the back, right sides together, and stitch the shoulder seams. Press the seams apart. Turn seams on the centre front pieces and stitch them on the machine or sew them by hand. Then edge neck and armholes with bias binding. Allow a piece of bias binding to extend on both sides at the front of the neck for tying. Work the ends into narrow ribbons using small stitches. Stitch the side seams and press the seams apart. Tack the seam at the bottom onto the reverse. Make a seam at the bottom and sides of the frill. Then stitch them by machine. Sew two gathering threads beside one another at the top of the frill. Use the largest stitches on the machine. Pull the gathering threads until the length of the frill fits the width of the night-dress at the bottom.
Tack the frill to the night-dress and stitch it on by machine from the right side. Neaten the seams with overcasting stitch.

Suggestions for other dolls' clothes
Many different dolls' clothes can be made from the basic shapes on pages 103 – 105.
The clothes can be fastened at the front instead of at the back, and they can be made longer and shorter, etc.

USING STRING AND FISHING LINE

Picture of a lion

The friendly lion among the flowers is worked on hessian with fishing line and various kinds of string. You can buy fishing line from fishing tackle shops. Pattern on page 106.

In this embroidery, we have tried to get various fabric effects.

We have not used a variety of colours, but only white and natural. To make the embroidery more alive, yarns of various thicknesses have been used.

Stitches: Rya stitch has been used for the lion's mane and tail switch as well as for the loops around the flowers. The stitches on mane and tail were then cut open. The edging around the lion's body, flower stems and rings are worked in couching, and the leaves in vandyke stitch.

The rings of thick string for the nose and the centre of the flowers were first sewn together as shown on page 68 and then sewn on the fabric.

The eyes are of brown felt and have been glued on. The eyelashes are in buttonhole stitch.

The body is filled out with string by stitching up and down into the fabric using tacking stitches not pulled quite tight. The lion can be mounted for hanging as shown on page 87.

The cushion cover below

The flowers on the cushion cover are made in the same way as the lion picture. The thick white cords are first sewn on by couching. The ends are pulled through to the reverse side. A row of Rya loops is then sewn around these with thin fishing line. Finally, the spirals in the centre are sewn together as shown on page 68 and then sewn on the fabric.

Pattern on page 107.

CORDS

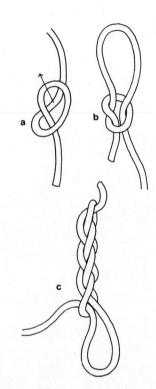

Finger crochet work using one end

a and b. First make a loop in one end of the thread in the same way as when making the first stitch for knitting. Hold the short end and use the other end to tighten the loop.

Place the fixed end around a hook, door handle, etc.

c. Hold the end for tightening the loop in the left hand. Lead the right thumb and index finger through the loop, take hold of the thread end from the left hand and pull it through the loop to form a new loop. Draw the first loop together. Continue in this way until the cord has reached the desired length. To finish off the cord, pull the final end through the loop.

Finger crochet work with two ends

You will need a thread about 8 times as long as the desired cord, plus 20 – 25 cm (8 – 10 ins).

First make a loop in the middle of the thread (see drawings a and b above for finger crochet work with one thread).

Place the loop on the left index finger and hold the knot with the thumb and middle finger. The thread for drawing the loop together must be on the left.

Now insert the right index finger into the loop and fish out the right-hand thread end so that a new loop is formed.

Change over so that the right thumb and middle finger hold the knot; allow the loop to slide off the left

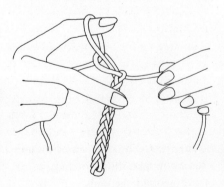

index finger and draw the loop together with the left hand. Then continue, fishing out the left-hand thread end with the left index finger to form a new loop; change the knot over to the left hand, allow the loop to slide off the right index finger and draw the loop together with the right hand. Continue in this way until the cord has reached the desired length. Finish off by pulling the final end through the loop.

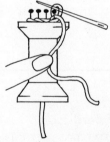

Horse's Rein ('knitting woman')

A horse's rein is worked on a cotton reel provided with 4 or 5 nails (with round heads). The nails must be near the centre hole of the reel if you want the rein to be tight and firm, and farther towards the edge if you want it to be loose and open.

Start by pulling the thread down through the hole in the reel, leaving the end free. Then place the thread around the nails in loops as shown in the drawing.

Next, place the thread around the next nail (to the left) above the loop and lift the loop over the thread and the nail with a darning needle, with a blunt point, or a sharpened stick. This forms a new loop.

Carry on in this way by placing the thread around one nail at a time (always towards the left) and pulling the loop on the nail over the thread and the nail.

The rein will then slowly grow out of the hole at the bottom of the reel. Pull it down now and again so that it is tightened.

When the rein is complete, pull the final end through each loop. It can be made more rigid by putting a cord inside it.

Twisted cord

For a twisted cord, use a thread about 6 times as long as you wish the finished cord to be.

Double the thread and tie the ends in a knot. Place the end with the knot on a hook, with a knitting needle or a pencil in the loop at the other end. Now twist the thread until it is quite tight by turning the knitting needle round and round.

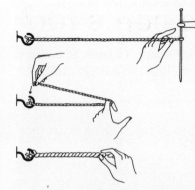

Then take hold of the middle of the twisted thread, put the ends together and allow the thread to twist together. Smooth over with the fingers so that any bulges and loops are evened out.

Braiding with three ends

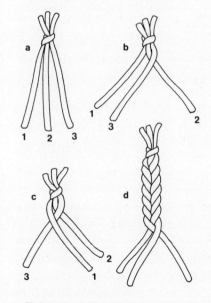

a. Take three threads and tie them together in a knot or tie a thin, strong thread around the ends.

b. Place the right thread (3) across the centre thread (2).

c. Place the left thread (1) across the centre thread (now 3).

d. Carry on in this way by placing the right and left threads alternately across the centre thread.

Braiding with four ends

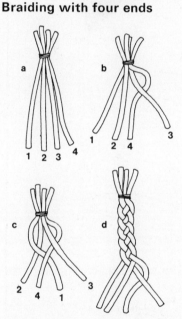

a. Take four threads and tie them together in a knot or tie a thin, strong thread around the ends.

b. Place the thread at the extreme right (4) under the next adjacent thread (3).

c. Place the thread on the extreme left (1) across the next (2) and under the next thread (now 4).

d. Carry on in this way until the braiding is the length you wish.

What can we use cords for?

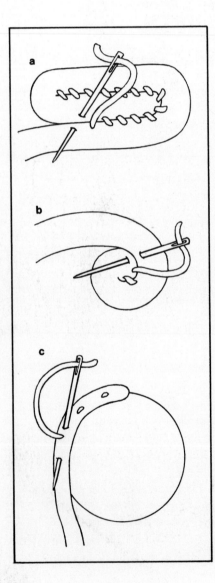

It is fun to make cords, but it is better to be able to use them for something. And there are many possibilities. For example: finishing off the edge of a cushion, wall hanging or handbag, for a hair band, a belt, a pendant for keys, coloured shoe laces, a picture carpet, decorative edges and decorations on articles such as an etui or a pencil case. From raffia you can make little mats for glasses or bottles, small baskets or a little doll's bed.

a. Cords may be sewn together as shown here if you want an oval shape.

b. This is how you work if you want a circle.

c. If you wish to sew cords onto fabric, you should select a material with a weave open enough for the cord to be pulled through.

First draw the outline of the shape to be made with a sharp pencil. Then pull one end of the cord through to the reverse side with a crochet hook or a large darning needle. Sew the end to the reverse with a thinner thread (such as sewing silk) and cut off short.

Stitch up into the right side and, as shown in the drawing, work a small stitch back down through cord and fabric and up a little farther ahead.

If you use a thin thread of the same colour as the cord the sewing will be invisible.

When the shape is covered, pull the other end of the cord through to the reverse, sew down and cut off short.

The wall carpet

You can make a complete picture by sewing cords onto fabric, then decorate this with a little embroidery. The cords may either be sewn directly on the fabric as shown in Fig. c or ovals and circles can be made as shown in Figs. a and b and then sewn on the fabric at the circumference. Thin embroidery cotton on a coarse linen was used here.
Pattern on page 109.

The pencil case

A pencil case made of hessian may be decorated with cords of different colours. See instructions on page 88.

The etui

Cords in circles inside one another may be sewn on hessian and made into an etui for such things as lighters or powder compacts.
See instructions on page 86.

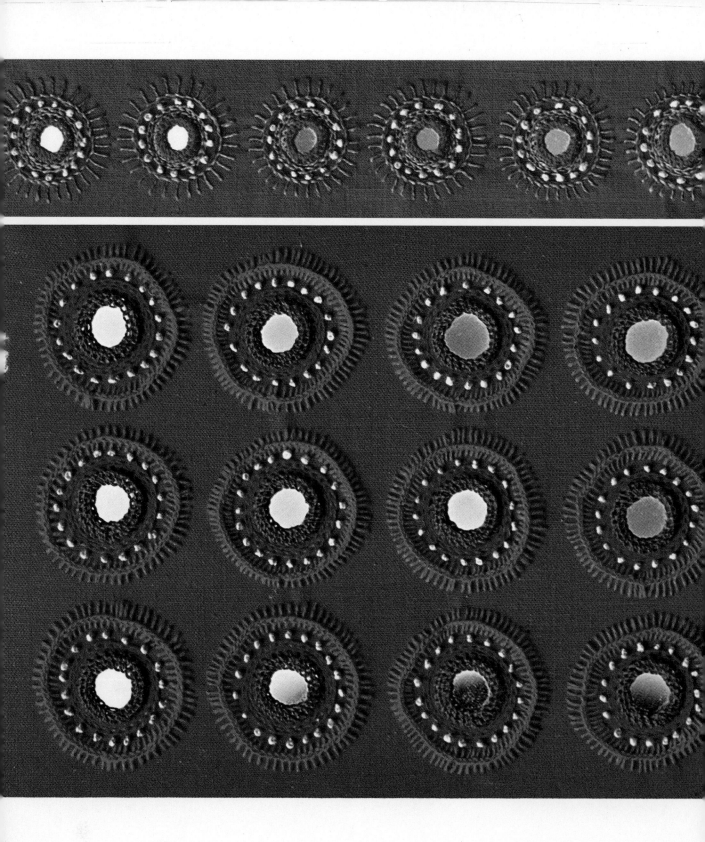

MIRROR EMBROIDERY

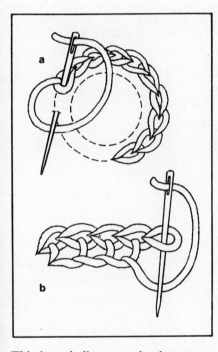

This is a challenge to the dexterous. The method is quite simple and you should not give in if the first attempt fails. All you need is some material, sequins and yarn. Use fairly large sequins as they are easier to work with.

Method

a. Work a row of chain stitches in a ring a little larger than the sequin. The inner dotted line in the drawing indicates the size of the sequin.

b. Sew a row of buttonhole stitches into this ring of chain stitches. Do not cut off the yarn, but now put on the sequin and continue using buttonhole stitch round and round until the sequin is held in place. You may need three or four rounds of buttonhole stitch before the sequin fits securely. But if you use strong yarn two rounds should be sufficient.

A good tip

Start by embroidering the chain stitch rings and then the rest of the embroidery around them. Wait until last to sew on the sequins with buttonhole stitch.

The ribbon

The ribbon is embroidered using linen yarn on orange-coloured cotton. The outer ring consists of a row of buttonhole stitches and then a row of French knots, followed by two rows of chain stitch. Finally three rows of buttonhole stitch, which secure the sequin, are sewn into the innermost row of chain stitches.
Use: The ribbon can be used as a hair band or as neck edging on a smock, etc.

The embroidered piece of material

The embroidery is worked with linen yarn on cotton. The outer row is worked in vandyke stitch (see page 44) followed by a row of French knots, and three rows of chain stitch. Finally (sewn into the inner row of chain stitches) three rows of buttonhole stitch hold the sequin in place.
Use: The mirror embroidery may be used for a handbag, waistcoat, yoke on a dress, cap, box lid, cushion, etc. See the suggestions for use on pages 80 – 89.

USING POTATO AND BRUSH

Fabric printing dyes may be used in a variety of ways; painting on fabric, potato cut printing, lino block printing, batik, tie-and-dye and many other forms. Two of the easiest types, as described in this book, are potato prints and painting on fabric. After printing the prints may, when dry, be embroidered by hand or machine if a richer effect is required.

Dyes

Many excellent fabric dyes are available, such as Polyprint, Printex and Rowney's Fabric Dyes, which can be bought from art shops. The first two consist of a colour that needs to be mixed with a binder and the last is ready mixed for use.

After printing, allow the print to dry and iron (set at a heat appropriate to the fabric used) on the reverse to fix the dye. Manufacturers supply full instructions with their dyestuffs. You will only require white, black and the three basic colours, yellow, blue and red. From these you can mix all the other colours you require, e.g. 1 part red + 2 parts yellow for orange; 1 part blue + 1 part yellow gives green; 1 part blue + 1 part red gives purple; 1 part each basic colour gives brown. Experiment with mixing until you get the colours you want. For pale colours add white. Mix colours in jars or tins with lids or screw tops if you wish to keep them.

Fabrics

Old sheets are quite suitable for fabric printing, as are most types of bleached or unbleached cottons. These include calico, poplin, cambric, cotton satin, etc.

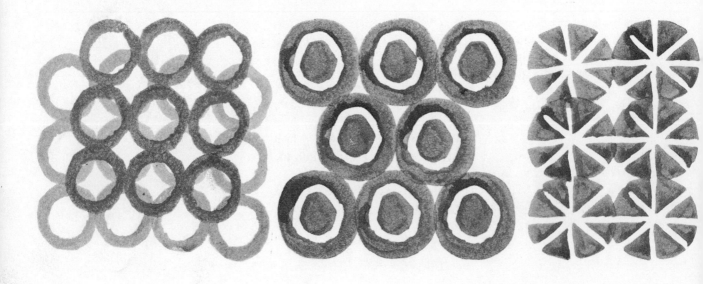

Any dressings should be removed from the fabric before printing by boiling in water with some washing soda added, then rinsed, dried and ironed flat.

Materials
—newspapers and old rag
—fabric for printing
—several brushes
—dyes
—jar containing cold water
—a thin piece of plastic foam or felt
—plastic bag
—washed potato
—dinner knife
—hair grip
—if possible, a cutting set or cutting knife.

Method
Spread the newspapers on the table and set out the various materials.

Preparing the Potato
Cut the potato in half, lengthways or across with the dinner knife and blot the cut half on the newspaper.

Use the hair grip or a cutting knife to cut a pattern on the cut surface (see the examples below); it is best to choose quite simple designs. Exciting effects may be obtained by over-printing, combining unusual colours and by embroidering on top.

Always try out your printing and any embroidery on sample pieces of cloth before starting the final work. Cut potatoes will keep for a day or so in a plastic bag; after that they will tend to shrink or go mouldy.

Printing
Place the thin piece of plastic foam or felt on a plastic bag and apply the dye with a brush. Press the cut surface of the potato on the dye-soaked pad and test your print on newspaper

Here are examples of potato printing on paper with quite simple designs made up in various ways.

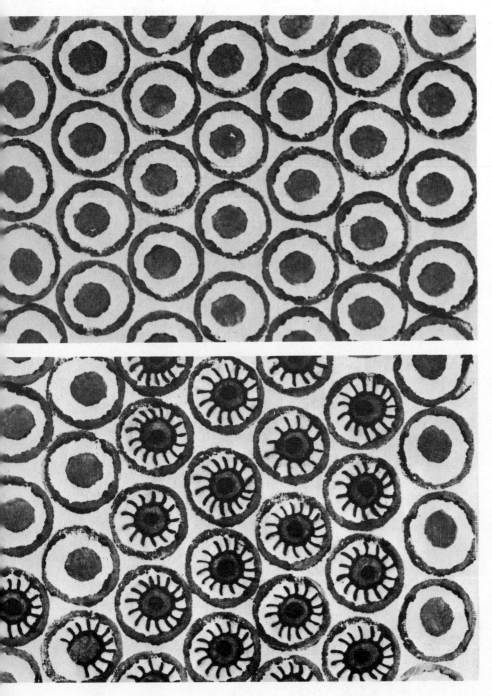

and a sample piece of fabric. Then, if satisfactory, print on the fabric and allow to dry.

You can also apply the dye directly to the potato, but care must be taken that it is applied evenly. The prints in this book are made in this way.

You can get amusing effects by overprinting, that is to say, printing on top of prints already made. Overprinting is most effective if the first print has been allowed to dry before applying the next.

Before and after

The illustrations on the left show the same piece of fabric with and without embroidery.

The design is printed with quite a simple potato block in lilac and later embroidered in purple with a thin linen yarn.

Stitches: buttonhole stitch and wheels of buttonhole stitch. The embroidered piece is suitable for a purse, handbag, cushion, etc.

The sun

The sun is intended as a door nameplate. The rays are printed using potato printing and the rest is painted. Finally, herring-bone stitch has been embroidered across the rays, stem stitch around the sun and mouth and buttonhole stitch around the eyes.

Embroidery wool was used. See instructions for mounting door nameplates on page 85.

Painting on fabric

House in landscape

The gay picture with the house, flowers, a rain shower, birds, etc., was painted and printed by a little girl. The top of the tree and the roof were printed using potato printing and the rest was painted. Finally, drawing was added with a waterproof felt-tip pen (spirit-based markers are very good). Felt-tip pen water colours are not suitable.

Materials

—newspapers and old rag
—dyes
—fabric for printing
—several brushes
—jar containing cold water

Method

Spread flat newspapers on the table and have dyes and water ready. Place the fabric as flat as possible on the newspaper.

Very lightly draw a design with pencil on the fabric and start to colour. Rinse the brush carefully in water and dry it with the rag each time the colour is changed. It is advisable to have a brush for each colour. Make sure there is no water in the brush after rinsing; the dyes may easily run if they become too diluted. Unless special effects using colours running together are wanted, this is not desirable.

You will get the strongest colours and the most even shapes by allowing one colour to dry before applying the next. When the work is finished, leave to dry and then iron on the reverse side with a hot iron.

Painting on fabric plus embroidery

You will see on the right various examples of fabric painting combined with embroidery. Only the small pin cushion at the bottom right is printed by potato printing.

Door Nameplate

The door nameplate was first painted, then embroidered and finally mounted. Both front and back are embroidered. The letters are embroidered in vandyke stitch. The junction between the two colours is worked in chain stitch. Double, thin cotton yarn has been used. See mounting and other suggestions for door nameplates on page 85.

Fish

The fish is intended as a mascot for someone born under Pisces. If you are born under another sign, you can make your own symbol. The symbols may also be used for pin cushions. Pattern for the fish is on page 114.
Not as many colours as you may think have been used for the fish, but by allowing the colours to run into one another an unusual variety of shades have appeared. Remember that each colour must be allowed to dry before the next is applied. The back of the fish is also painted.
Mounting: Place front and back right sides together. Stitch by machine all round except at top or bottom, where an opening must be left. Turn the right side out and stuff the fish with kapok or other filling. Sew up the opening.

Small wall hanging

The wall hanging was made by Anne Marie. She first painted the hanging, then worked the embroidery. The finished embroidery was then backed with iron-on Vilene, but only on the back of the picture itself. The surplus seams were turned round the Vilene on the reverse and glued down. Finally, she sewed on two sticks at the top and bottom and fixed a hanging thread.

Purse

The exciting purse with gold embroidery was designed and worked by a 13-year-old girl. She first sketched some ideas using water colour and gold paint. Then she chose one of the ideas and transferred it to fabric. The pattern is on page 115. She painted the same places several times over to get strong colours. She also painted a brown background.
The gold embroidery was worked in stem stitch, apart from the rays of the eyes which are in buttonhole stitch. Gold metallic thread can be bought in embroidery shops and in needlework departments of large stores.
Mounting: Iron-on Vilene was applied to the back of both parts. The parts were placed right sides together and stitched by machine around the edge, except for a large section at the top. The seams were trimmed down and the right side turned out. The zip was first tacked, and then sewn on with back stitch from the right side.

Pin cushion

The pin cushion was printed using potato printing with a simple round block. Printing was first done in yellow in the centre, and then in orange in a circle around this. Finally an outer row of circles in red was printed. The colours were dry before the next layer was printed over them. The embroidery was worked in French knots in the centre, chain stitch (double thread) in a ring around this and stem stitch in rings on the outer circles.
Mounting, see page 84.

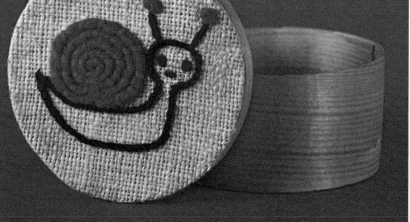

USE AND MOUNTING

A number of uses for embroidery, together with instructions for mounting, are described on the following pages.

Easter hen with chicks
The hen is intended to keep eggs warm. Line a basket with a flat cushion filled with wadding.

Materials
About 55 × 80 cm (22 × 32 ins) cotton fabric for the hen and chicks; thin, pink poplin or cotton for the hearts, comb and wattle; 20 × 25 cm (8 × 10 ins) of orange felt for the beaks and the bases of the chicks; iron-on Vilene for the eyes; kapok for stuffing the chicks; embroidery cotton in various colours. The lining for the hen needs two pieces of quilted material, each 24 × 30 cm (10 × 12 ins).

The pattern is on page 122. Trace the pattern pieces onto transparent paper and transfer to the fabric.

The hen
Cut out two pieces for the hen and sew up the incisions. Then work the embroidery on both sides. All the rings are worked in chain stitch and rays are embroidered around the small rings. The white dots are French knots. The heart is cut out and appliquéd on and the eyes are circles of iron-on Vilene. Embroider two rows of chain stitch around the eyes after ironing on, and fill in the pupils with satin stitch.

The comb and wattle are cut double, sewn and turned right side out. The beak is cut from orange felt.

When all the embroidery has been completed and pressed, and the comb, wattle and beak are ready, sew the parts together. Beak, comb and wattle are placed between the two sections of the hen, which are laid right sides together, and then sewn on the machine. Turn right side out. Sew the lining, which is cut from the pattern for the hen, and place inside. Turn up the outside material of the hen 2 cm (¾ in) at the bottom and sew to the lining with small stitches.

The chicks
Cut out the pattern pieces for the chicks, allowing 1 cm (½ in) for seams and cutting two pieces for the body. Sew the eyes as for the hen. The pupils can be placed in different positions so that the chicks are looking up or down or to one side. Cut the base and the beak from orange felt. Then work the embroidery. Glue on the heart. Place front and back right sides together, with the comb between and perhaps also the beak (if you want to make a chick in profile). Sew by hand and turn right side out. Turn up the hem at the bottom, stuff the chick with kapok and sew the felt bottom to the body using small stitches.

Box with embroidery
You can decorate practically any kind of box with an embroidered design. Trace the outline of the lid and add 1 cm (½ in) to the shape all round.

Cut out the material and work the embroidery. It may be a flower, a border around the edge or, as here, a snail (see photograph on page 41 and pattern on page 111).

Lay a piece of cardboard the size of the lid on the back of the embroidery. Then turn up the seam around the cardboard and glue on. Then glue the part to the lid. If the box is a wooden one, it can be painted or stained to a colour matching the embroidery. In that case, this must be done before the embroidery is glued on.

Cushions
Make the cushions large, small, oblong or round. Place tassels at the

corners or sew a loop in one corner. Before starting to embroider a cushion cover, it is as well to decide on the cushion that is to be put inside the cover. Perhaps you have an old one that needs a new cover; otherwise they can be bought new in various sizes and with different fillings.

Make the cushion cover a little smaller than the cushion itself, so that you get a nice, smooth fit. Cut two pieces to the size decided upon plus 1 cm ($\frac{1}{2}$ in) for seams all round. You can perhaps cut one long piece, which is then folded in the middle; this means that there are only three seams. The decoration may be an embroidery, appliqué work, fabric printing, etc. See the other pages in the book. When the embroidery is finished and

pressed, sew the cushion together by machine. Leave an opening at the bottom large enough to allow the cushion to be pushed through. Trim the seams and turn right side out. Tack along the edges to finish corners and sides neatly. Press carefully and pull out the tacking thread.

Place the cushion in the cover and sew up the opening using small hemming stitches (see page 90). You may also sew in a zip instead.

If you want a further edge around the cushion, braid or twist a cord according to the instructions on pages 66 – 67 and sew on.

Boxes you make yourself

Boxes can be used for many things such as sewing materials, jewellery, as a beauty-box with a mirror or as a secret box with curtain rings sewn on which can be locked at the front with a padlock. The embroidery is worked before the box is made up. Remember that the fabric must be twice as large as the size of the lid (see drawing b).

a. For a box with a lid, pieces of cardboard must be used as base, lid and four sides. The lid must be a fraction larger than the base.

b. Then cover the cardboard pieces with fabric. Use for each piece of cardboard a piece of fabric twice as large as the cardboard plus enough for seams.

Lay the cardboard on the fabric as shown in the drawing and glue the edges around it on three sides. Take

care not to apply too much glue at the extreme edges, as sewing will later be carried out here and it is difficult to work through glue. A thin piece of foam rubber may be placed under the cardboard so that the box becomes nicely soft.

c. Fold down the fabric, tack the seam on the reverse and sew along the edges using oversewing stitch.

d. When all pieces have been covered with fabric, sew them together, using oversewing stitch, to make a box.

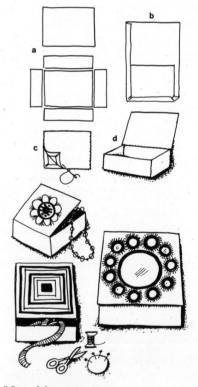

Matchboxes, etc.

Matchboxes can be finished in various ways. Fabrics that do not fray (such as felt) can be glued directly on the

box. See the matchboxes on page 57. To decorate the boxes you may use fabric printing, appliqué, embroidery, etc.

Most fabrics fray and so we must work in the following manner:

Take a piece of card the size of the box, or a fraction larger if you wish the cover to extend a little beyond the edges. Lay the embroidery, which must be the size of the piece of card plus 1 cm ($\frac{1}{2}$ in) seam allowance for turning over all round, with the reverse side facing upwards and place the piece of card on top. Fold up the turn-over around the card and glue on. The whole is then glued to the matchbox. Make both a top and a bottom – the bottom without embroidery – so that the box is not accidentally opened upside-down. A cigar box may be mounted in the same manner. The box may perhaps be painted in a colour to match the embroidery.

Fireplace glove

A fireplace glove is easy to make from felt. It may be decorated with a sweep, also of felt, and glued on. The face, etc., is embroidered with a thin embroidery cotton. See photograph on page 57 and the patterns on pages 96 and 125.

You may also choose other felt designs, or use embroidery only for decoration. Make up your own design or take ideas from other pages in this book.

Method: Trace the glove pattern onto transparent paper. Lay the pattern on the fabric and allow $\frac{1}{2}$ cm ($\frac{1}{4}$ in) for the seam, except at the wrist edge of the glove where $1\frac{1}{2}$ cm ($\frac{1}{2}$ in) must be allowed. Cut out two pieces.

Work the decoration. Then place the two sections right sides together, and sew by machine. Turn right side out and turn over the hem at the wrist edge of the glove. Glue it or sew along it using herring-bone stitch. Sew on a loop.

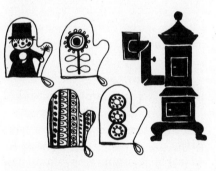

Face cloths

Using the pattern for the fireplace glove on page 96, you can make attractive face cloths for the entire family from all the beautiful towelling colours available in the shops. Cut out two pieces.

You can use appliqué in colours different from the glove to decorate the towelling. Zig-zag the shapes using the sewing machine or sew on

as shown on page 51. Embroidery looks pretty on towelling, but a little care must be taken that you do not pull the loops of the towelling while sewing.

When the embroidery is finished, place the two sections right sides together, and join by machine. Trim the seams and neaten them using overcasting stitch or use zig-zag stitch on the machine.

Edge the top with bias binding ending in a loop. (Edging with bias binding, see page 91.)

Spectacles case

If you wish to make a spectacles case, you must first decide how large it is to be. The size of glasses varies greatly. You can perhaps use the pattern on page 97 as a basis, making it larger or smaller.

Here are instructions for a very simple spectacles case. It is cut in two pieces from the pattern, allowing 1 cm ($\frac{1}{2}$ in) for seams. Work the embroidery and iron onto the reverse

sides two pieces of iron-on Vilene the size of the case (without seams).

Then place the pieces right sides together, and stitch around the sides and at bottom. Trim the seams and neaten them with overcasting stitch. Turn over the hem at the top onto the reverse and secure with herring-bone stitch.

Bookcover

You can make school books, guest books, scrap books, photograph

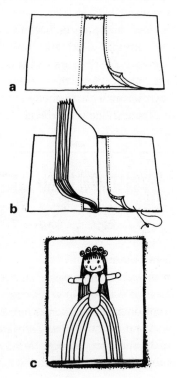

albums and loose-leaf books for recipes or other cuttings look prettier. The cover is made from a long piece of material, in either end of which pockets are made for inserting the book cover. The width of the fabric must be the height of the book plus seams, and the length must be sufficient for two pockets.

a. When the embroidery is finished and pressed, make a hem at both ends. This is sewn by machine or by hand. Turn down hems at top and bottom edges, fold the material inwards to form two pockets, and sew with small oversewing stitches. (Leave the bottom right-hand seam open.) Sew the seams at the top and bottom between the pockets (where the spine of the book will be) with herring-bone stitch.

b. Place the book in the cover and sew up the last seam with oversewing stitch.

c. The finished cover.

Bib

A dribbling or feeding bib is best made of thin towelling edged with bias binding. There are patterns for two different bibs on page 96.

First edge the bib all round, except for the neck. Then edge the neck, leaving a piece of bias binding extending on both sides for tying. Sew the tying ribbon together by hand with small stitches to make a narrow cord.

Trace the design – a sun, a border,

etc. – on the bib and embroider. You may also sew on a towelling figure of a different colour by zig-zag stitches on the machine. It may then be decorated with embroidery.

Pin cushions

You do not need much fabric for a pin cushion, and it can be made from many kinds of remnant provided the needle can be pushed through. For example, felt and linen are excellent. They can be made in various shapes and sizes. The pin cushion on page 23 measures 14×14 cm ($5\frac{1}{2} \times 5\frac{1}{2}$ ins).

A good small size is 8×8 cm (3×3 ins). Cut out front and back pieces to the measurements desired plus 1 cm ($\frac{1}{2}$ in) for seams. Embroider the front and press. Lay the sections right sides together and stitch by hand on three sides. Turn right side out and stuff the cushion with kapok or other filling. Sew up the last side, perhaps providing a loop.

Bathing wrap for a baby or doll

A towelling bathing wrap with an embroidered edge is easy to make from a triangle and a square. The whole article is edged with bias binding. The measurements given in the drawing apply to a baby or a large doll. If you wish to make the wrap for a smaller doll, try out fabric remnants until the correct size of triangle and square is found.

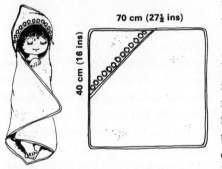

70 cm (27¼ ins)

40 cm (16 ins)

First edge the hood with bias binding along the longest side of the triangle. Then embroider the border. You may get some ideas from pages 16–19.

Lay the triangle right side up on one corner of the square. Edge the wrap all round with bias binding, sewing on the hood at the same time (tack on first).

Nameplates for doors

Cotton is very good for making nameplates for doors. The width may, for example, be 6 cm (2½ ins), and the length depends upon the length of the name.

Various types of decoration can be used for nameplates. They may be completely embroidered; you may use appliqué with embroidery; or, as shown on page 79, you may colour them with fabric printing dyes and then embroider.

Method 1

You need only a front section and iron-on Vilene for the back for this method. When the embroidery is finished and pressed, tack the hem on the reverse. Iron carefully along the edges and pull out the tacking thread. Iron a piece of iron-on Vilene (without seam) to the back.

Provide a loop at the top so that the nameplate can hang.

Method 2

You need an embroidered front, a back and a piece of iron-on Vilene for Method 2. Iron a piece of iron-on Vilene, without seam, on the back of the finished embroidery. Tack the hem of the embroidery on the reverse. The piece for the back cover must have a hem of about 1 cm (½ in). Tack the hem on the reverse and lay the back against the front, wrong sides together. Then sew the parts together by hand using oversewing stitch. Make a loop at the top.

You can also lay the sections right sides together (without tacking the hem on the reverse), stitch them on the machine except for an opening, turn right side out and sew up the opening with oversewing stitch.

Tray ribbons

A tray ribbon is made from two ribbons sewn around a ring. Two pieces of material, each 10 cm (4 ins) wide and 82 cm (33 ins) long, are needed for ribbons about 4 cm (1½ ins) wide and 80 cm (32 ins) long.

a. Work the embroidery on the centre 4 cm (1½ ins) of the material. Then pass the ends through the ring and sew together by machine. Press the seams.

b. Tack the seams on both sides onto the reverse. Fold the ribbons as shown in the drawing and tack down the edges. Sew the centre seam together with small stitches.

c. The finished tray ribbon.

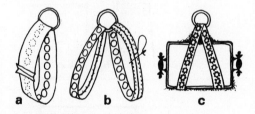

a b c

Tea cosies

You can quite easily make the finished stuffing for a tea cosy from a cotton material, such as calico, and wadding. Cut two pieces of wadding, of the appropriate shape, without any seam allowance. Next cut two pieces

of calico, which should be twice as long as the wadding, and allow 1 cm ($\frac{1}{2}$ in) for seams. Fold each piece of calico round each piece of wadding, turn in the edges and tack round. Then lay the two sections together and join the curved edges using oversewing stitch.

Suitable fabrics for the outer cover include cotton and linen.

Rounded tea cosy

Using the shape of your finished stuffing as a guide, cut out two pieces of material for the outer cover. Allow 1 cm ($\frac{1}{2}$ in) for the seams and hem. Work the embroidery, using your own design or find one among the patterns at the back of the book. For a loop cut out a small strip of material, fold it in half and hem it by hand.

Place the two sides of the outer cover right sides together, tacking the loop in position at the same time. Join the curved edges on the machine or use oversewing stitch. Turn right side out and place over the finished stuffing. You can sew the bottom of the stuffing to the bottom of the outer cover, but it is best not to do

this. The outer cover can then be easily taken off and washed when it gets dirty.

You can make tea cosies of all sorts of different shapes by varying the pattern you start with.

Etui with cord embroidery

from page 69

Materials:

A piece of hessian, a good 7 cm ($2\frac{3}{4}$ ins) wide and 26 cm (10 ins) long.

Lining fabric of a colour matching the cord embroidery (here turquoise), 7×26 cm ($2\frac{3}{4} \times 10$ ins).

Wool for cords.

Sewing silk.

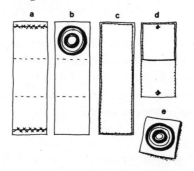

a and b. Turn up 1 cm ($\frac{1}{2}$ in) all round the hessian and secure the hem using herring-bone stitch. Sew the cords onto one-third of the hessian.

c. From the front of the lining, turn over a good 1 cm ($\frac{1}{2}$ in) to the reverse side all round. The piece should be slightly smaller than the hessian.

Place lining and hessian wrong sides together and tack along the edges. Then sew on the lining using small stitches. Take care that the stitches

do not go through to the right side of the hessian. The lining may be left out.

d. Fold up the lower third of the hessian (right side facing outwards) so that a pocket is formed and sew both sides using oversewing stitch.

A snap fastener may be sewn on at the bottom of the flap.

The etui can be used for a lighter, powder compact and lipstick, loose change, etc.

Collars

A tightly woven cotton, white or coloured, is a good choice for a decorative collar. You will need a piece about 18×40 cm (7×16 ins). There is a pattern for a collar on page 96. You can choose either the rounded or pointed design. Trace the pattern and see whether it fits. If the collar is too large, it can be made a little smaller by making a fold in the centre at the back. If it is too small, add a piece. Cut out two pieces. Work the embroidery on one of these; this can be a border along the edge, a single ring or a flower at the front, etc. Press the finished embroidery

from the reverse using a damp cloth. Then lay the two pieces right sides together, and stitch them by machine all round except for 12 cm (5 ins) at the top of the collar at the rear centre. Trim the seams and turn right side out. Sew up the opening by hand using oversewing stitch. At the front of the collar, sew a hook onto one side and an eye onto the other.

Wall hangings

Wall hangings can be mounted in various ways:

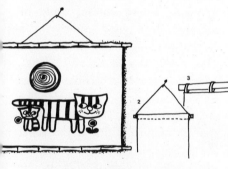

1. Hanging pictures on bamboo sticks

Hem the finished embroidery on all sides. A piece of iron-on Vilene may be ironed on the back before the hems are turned over to make it more rigid. Then sew on bamboo sticks at the top and bottom, by sewing around the stick at intervals of about 5 cm (2 ins). Finally, sew on a hanging loop.

2. Hanging by means of a channel

You can also make channels at the top and bottom through which the sticks are then pushed. Tie the hang-ing thread to the ends of the top stick.

3. Hanging by means of loops

Loops can be made from narrow ribbons – perhaps bias binding – and sewn on at the top and bottom of the wall hanging. Then push in the sticks and fasten the hanging thread to the top stick.

Pot holders

Pot holders can be made from felt, cotton, etc. If they are made from cotton, it is as well to place a piece of flannelette between the layers.

There are patterns on page 97 for three different kinds of pot holder: round, square and heart-shaped. For a pot holder, cut two pieces of fabric plus 1 cm ($\frac{1}{2}$ in) for the seam and one piece of flannelette – also with 1 cm ($\frac{1}{2}$ in) for seams. Work the embroidery and press. You may perhaps find ideas from the designs on pages 16-21 or among the patterns at the back of the book.

Make a loop – perhaps from bias binding.

Lay the front and back right sides together. Lay the flannelette on top and stitch the three pieces by machine all round except for a section of about 10 cm (4 ins). Sew the loop on at the same time. Trim the seam and turn right side out. Sew the last 10 cm (4 ins) by hand using small stitches. If necessary, stitch the edge by machine to get it quite flat.

You may also place the pieces (here without a seam allowance) together, right side out, with the piece of flannelette in between and then edge all round with bias binding.

For felt pot holders the seam allow-ance can be omitted and the parts sewn together, right side out, using buttonhole stitch.

Hair band

On page 18 there are various sugges-tions for trimmings that can be used as hair bands.

You need for a hair band of 45 × 3 cm (18 × 1 ins) a piece of fabric 47 × 8 cm (19 × 3 ins). Work the embroidery on the 3 cm (1 in) in the centre. Then tack the hem 1 cm ($\frac{1}{2}$ in) on the reverse. Fold the material to form a narrow ribbon with a seam in the centre at the back (see the tray

ribbons on page 85). Sew the seam together by hand using small stitches. Join the ends with a piece of elastic.

Pencil case

from page 69

For the pencil case you need two pieces of hessian, each 22×7 cm ($9 \times 2\frac{3}{4}$ ins), one zip fastener and finger-crocheted and plaited cords of wool. Sew the cords to the hessian, perhaps on both pieces. Lay the two pieces right sides together and stitch three sides by machine. Neaten the seams with overcasting stitch and turn right side out. First tack on the zip fastener and then sew it on by hand using small back stitch, as shown in Fig. p on page 93.

Napkin rings

For a napkin ring of 12×3 cm (5×1 ins), use a piece of material 14×8 cm (6×3 ins). Work the embroidery on the 3 cm (1 in) in the centre. Tack the hem allowance, 1 cm ($\frac{1}{2}$ in), on the reverse side. Fold the material to form a 3 cm (1 in) wide band with a seam at the centre back. See tray ribbons on page 85. Then join the seam using small stitches. Finally, hem the ends, also using small stitches. Sew tying ribbons to each end of the rings.

Bookmark

For a bookmark of 18×4 cm ($7 \times 1\frac{1}{2}$ ins), use a piece of material 20×10 cm (8×4 ins). Work the embroidery on the 4 cm ($1\frac{1}{2}$ ins) in the centre. Tack the hem allowance – 1 cm ($\frac{1}{2}$ in) – on the reverse side. Fold the material to form a 4 cm ($1\frac{1}{2}$ ins) wide ribbon with the seam in the centre back; see also tray ribbons on page 85. Then join the seam using small stitches. Finally, sew the ends by hand, also using small stitches. The bookmark may then perhaps be decorated with tassels (see page 22).

Egg basket

First, obtain a basket of suitable size. The size depends upon how many eggs will be held in the basket.

Make a cushion large enough to cover the bottom and sides of the basket. It may be stuffed with wadding.

Then trace the outline of the basket; this may be round, oval or square. Cut two pieces of material, allowing 1 cm ($\frac{1}{2}$ in) for the hems, and work embroidery on one piece. You may perhaps find a design among the patterns at the back of the book. Also cut a piece of wadding without hem allowance.

Lay front and back right sides together and stitch all round, except for about 12 cm (5 ins). Trim the seam and turn right side out. Insert the wadding and sew up the 12 cm (5 ins) by hand, using small stitches.

Egg cosies

There is a pattern for an egg cosy on page 97. You will need two pieces of material 11×11 cm ($4\frac{1}{4} \times 4\frac{1}{4}$ ins) for the cosy itself, two pieces of material about 10×10 cm (4×4 ins) for the lining and two pieces of thin foam rubber or wadding, also about 10×10 cm (4×4 ins).

Cut out two pieces for the outer cosy, allowing $\frac{1}{2}$ cm ($\frac{1}{4}$ in) for the seam around the top and 1 cm ($\frac{1}{2}$ in) at the bottom edge. Cut two pieces of foam rubber or wadding without seam allowance. For the lining, cut two pieces without seam allowance, except for the bottom edge where 1 cm ($\frac{1}{2}$ in) is allowed.

Work and press the embroidery.

Lay the front and back right sides together, and join the sections by hand or by machine. Turn right side out. Then sew together the two lining pieces. Insert the two pieces of foam rubber into the outer cosy and then insert the lining. Turn up the lining between the outer cosy and the foam rubber and join to the outer cosy with oversewing stitch all round.

Tablecloths and runners

Linen and cotton are suitable for tablecloths and runners. You must remember when choosing fabric and yarn that both will have to withstand repeated washing. You will see on page 18 how just one shape can be used in rows to form a complete pattern suitable for a tablecloth design. The shapes can be set in a row to form a runner, or in a circle as shown in the drawing of the round tablecloth on page 22.

How to work hems and corners, see page 92.

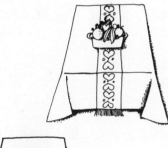

Memo pad

A memo pad can be useful in the kitchen and beside the telephone.

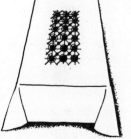

Method: Cut two pieces of cardboard (a little larger than the pad itself) for the front and back, and a piece for the spine matching the thickness of the pad.

Cut out the material for the cover allowing about $1\frac{1}{2}$ cm ($\frac{5}{8}$ in) for the hem when the cardboard sections are placed on it. Allow a very small space between the spine and the front and back; see drawing a.

Work the embroidery. It may perhaps be an embroidered or appliquéd cat as shown in the drawing (pattern, page 112). But you may prefer to make your own design.

a. Lay the embroidered cover face downwards and glue on the cardboard sections. The glue is applied to the cardboard pieces. Take care not to apply so much glue that blotches appear on the front of the embroidery. Turn over the edges of the material and glue to the cardboard. Allow the glue to dry completely.

b. Iron on a piece of iron-on Vilene a little smaller than the cover. Instead of this, a piece of felt or rigid paper may be glued on.

Sew a piece of material double to form a strip, about 3 cm (1 in) wide and as long as the width of the cover. Join the strip to the sides of the cover

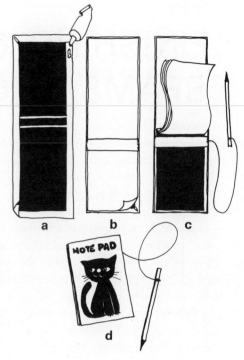

with small stitches. The strip is to keep the pad in place and must therefore be right above it. Test with the pad to see where the strip should be to keep it in place and to allow the cover to be closed.

c. Insert the cardboard back of the pad into the strip and sew a cord, with a pencil attached, to the side of the strip.

d. The finished pad.

FINISHING OF EDGES, SEAMS, ETC.

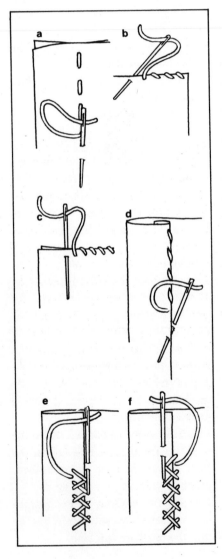

Tacking (running stitch)

a. Tacking is worked from the top downwards or from right to left. This stitch is used, for example, to join pieces before stitching by machine.

Overcasting and oversewing stitch

b. Overcasting stitch is worked from right to left. This stitch is used for neatening seams, to prevent the fabric from fraying.

c. Oversewing stitch is very similar and is used to join two pieces of material together.

Hemming

d. Hemming can be worked from the top downwards or from right to left. The needle is pushed in beneath a few threads in the fabric and up into the edge of the hem. It is important for the stitches in the fabric to be small, as otherwise they can be clearly seen from the right side.

Herring-bone stitch

e and f. Work is carried out from the bottom upwards, alternately on the right and left sides. A few threads are taken up alternately down into

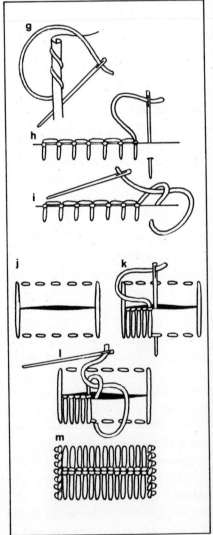

the fabric and up into the edge of the hem. Make sure that the thread is always laid on the correct side. (See page 45.)

e. Thread kept on the left and sewing carried out on the right.

f. the reverse of e.

Rolled hem

g. Roll the hem firmly with the left hand and sew across it using a whipping stitch. Work from the top downwards. This hem is suitable for very thin fabrics.

Blanket stitch

h and i. Blanket stitch is worked from left to right. The stitch is worked in two sections: first into the fabric from behind (h) and then from behind and into the loop formed (i). (See page 44.)

Buttonhole

j. A buttonhole must be as long as the width of the button plus 2 mm ($\frac{1}{16}$ in). First work running stitch around the buttonhole as shown in the drawing. Then cut the opening of the buttonhole. Now work buttonhole stitch from left to right. When one long side is finished, pull a few extra threads at the end and work buttonhole stitch across the threads so that a bar is formed. The stitches are not worked right through the material but only grip it very lightly so that the bar can move from side to side.

m. Then work the other long side and the other end in the same manner.

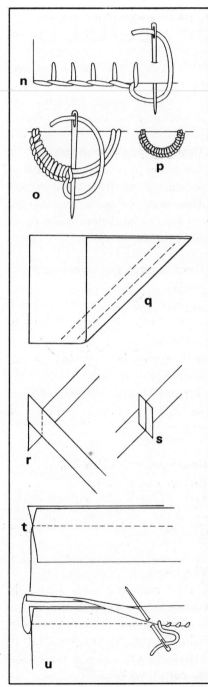

Buttonhole stitch

n. Buttonhole stitch is worked from left to right. Start by pushing the needle up into the edge and then push it in a little way up in the fabric. Then up again below the edge and over the thread. Pull the stitch straight down. (See page 44.)

Buttonhole loop

o. First sew loosely from side to side a few times at the width desired for the loop. Work tight buttonhole stitches across the threads.

p. The finished loop.

Edging with bias binding

Bias binding can be bought in many colours. If you cut it yourself, take care that it is completely on the bias and not merely 'almost' on the bias, as otherwise it may form folds when sewn.

q. *Cutting bias strips.* Fold the fabric as shown here and cut out the strips. If there is not enough material for one long strip to go all round the edge, several strips can be joined.

r. *Joining bias strips.* Lay two bias strips right sides together and at right angles to one another. Stitch by machine.

s. Press the seams apart.

t. *Edging with bias binding.* Place the binding with its right side against the right side of the edge to be finished. Stitch by hand or by machine.

u. Turn the binding to the reverse side and sew down with small stitches into the machine stitching.

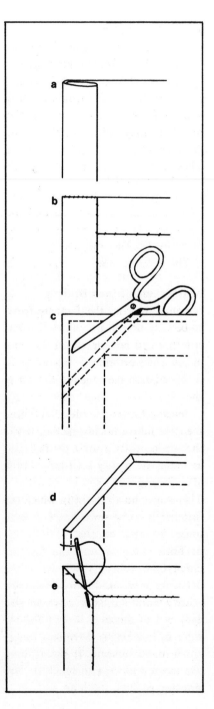

Finishing of corners

For thin fabrics, it is best to make the hems so that there are three layers of fabric in the whole width of the hem (see a).

b. If narrow hems are used, the corners may be sewn up fully as shown in b.

For thicker fabrics and wider hems – over 1½ cm ($\frac{5}{8}$ in) – the hems will be too clumsy and therefore one layer in the width of the hem is allowed plus ½ cm ($\frac{1}{4}$ in) for turn-over. It will also be an advantage to make mitred corners:

c. Cut off the corner.

d. Fold over the ½ cm ($\frac{1}{4}$ in) for the turn-over and press.

e. Turn down the hems and tack, then join using small stitches. Sew the corner on the right and left side alternately as shown.

Mitred corners can only be used where the hems are of equal width on all sides.

Hems worked with drawn thread hemstitch

Many pieces of work will look attractive if they are hemmed with drawn thread hemstitch.

The hems

f. First press the hems. Finish the corners as shown in drawings c, d and e, although here the turn-over must follow the thread accurately. Drawing f shows how the hem is tacked and the corner worked.

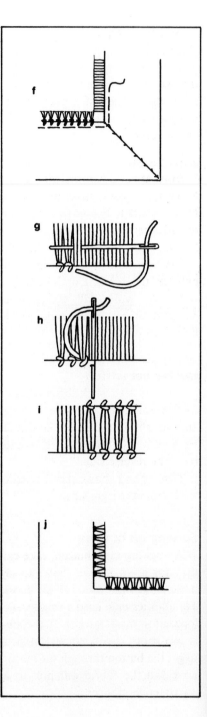

Drawing out threads

Draw out one or more (here two) threads just above the top edge of the hem. Cut the threads far enough from the corners for them to be threaded into a needle and fastened on the reverse.

Drawn thread hemstitch

g. This is worked from the reverse. Make a stitch behind a bundle of threads (here two threads).

h. Then stitch down into the edge of the hem (and into this only) and pull up the stitch. Continue in this way. The work will therefore be hemmed at the same time as the hemstitch is sewn.

Ladder hemstitch

i. You can also work the stitches on the opposite edge of the drawn thread and so obtain a ladder hemstitch. Here also the stitches are worked from the reverse side.

j. This shows how the hemstitch looks from the right side.

Sewing on buttons

When sewing on a button, take care that it is given a stem; that is to say, it stands a little clear of the fabric. Thin fabrics only need a small stem – longer for thick fabrics. If the stem is too short it will be very difficult to get the button through the button-hole, and the fabric will pull in an unattractive manner.

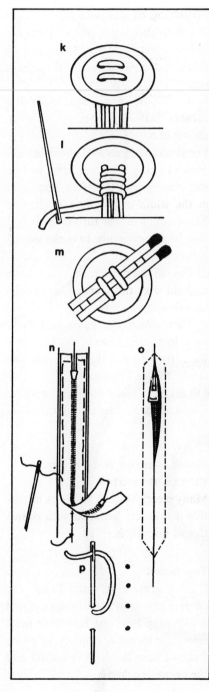

k. Hold the button a little away from the fabric and work the stitches so that they are of equal length.

l. When all stitches are worked, wind the thread around them. Finally, secure the end.

m. You may also work across matches or pins to make the stem. They can be easily removed afterwards.

Sewing on zip fasteners

A zip fastener must be sewn on so that a machine-sewn or hand-sewn row of stitching is on either side of it, far enough from the fastener for it to be easy to pull up and down. The stitching can be worked into a point at top and bottom.

n. First press the edges of the slit in the fabric and then tack on the fastener. This may be done on either the right side or the reverse side. Hold the fabric lightly against the fastener, as otherwise it may go astray a little after sewing on.

This shows how the slit in which the fastener is to be sewn has first been joined by small stitches.

o. Then stitch around the fastener either by machine as shown in the drawing, or by hand using small back stitch. Work the back stitch so that only a tiny stitch is visible on the right side, whereas there is a longer stitch on the reverse. It should look like small dots on the right side. See drawing p.

PATTERNS

All the patterns are same size but
have no seam allowance.

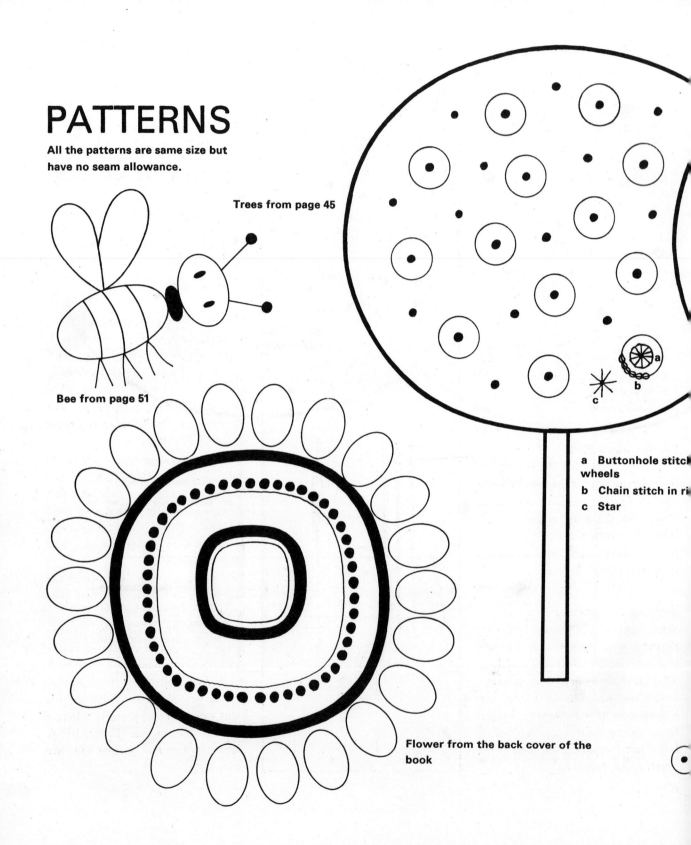

Trees from page 45

Bee from page 51

a Buttonhole stitch
wheels
b Chain stitch in ri
c Star

Flower from the back cover of the
book

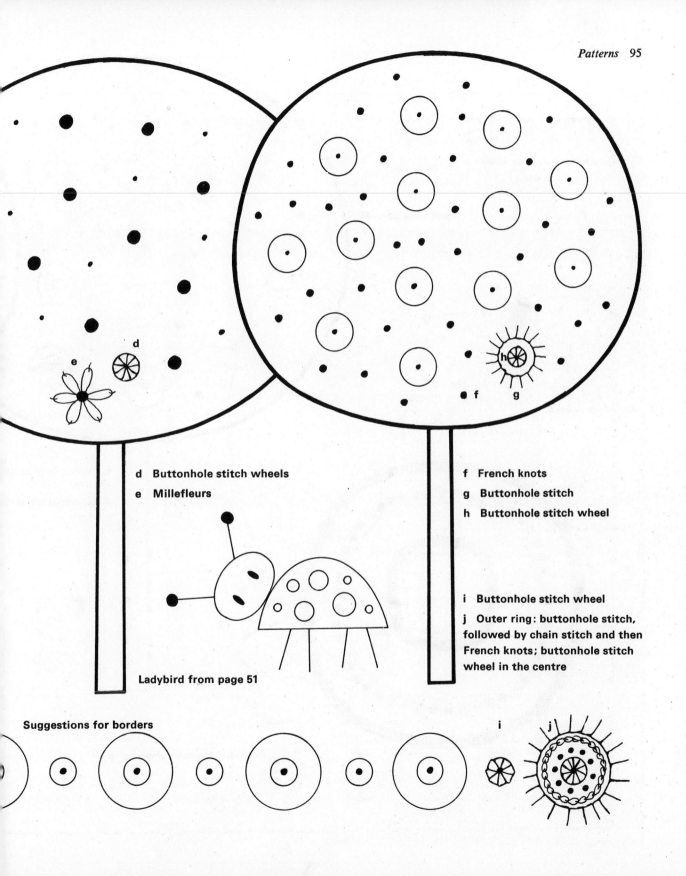

d   Buttonhole stitch wheels
e   Millefleurs

f   French knots
g   Buttonhole stitch
h   Buttonhole stitch wheel

i   Buttonhole stitch wheel
j   Outer ring: buttonhole stitch, followed by chain stitch and then French knots; buttonhole stitch wheel in the centre

Ladybird from page 51

Suggestions for borders

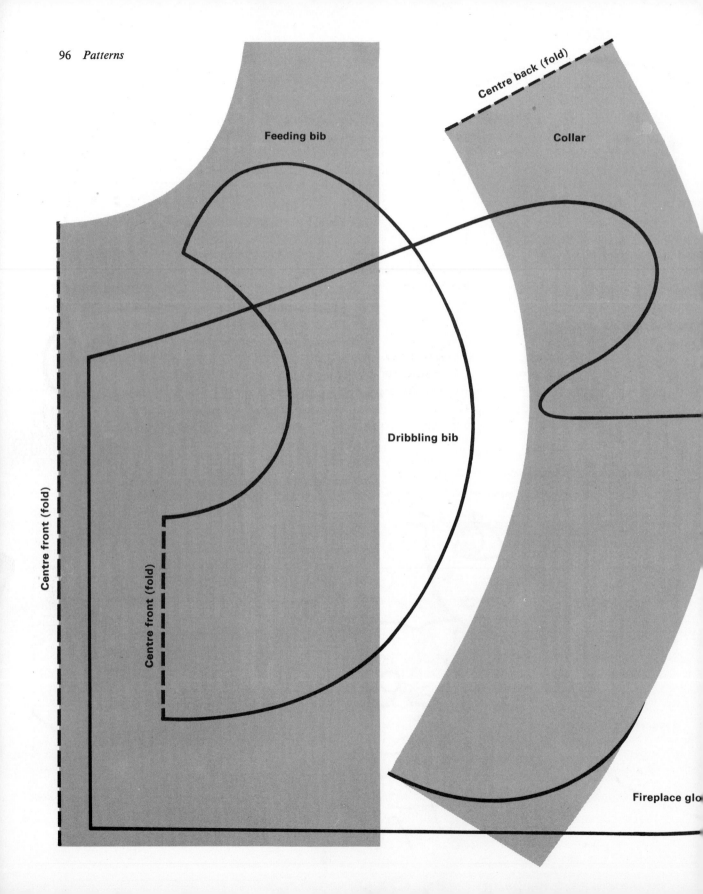

Feeding bib

Collar

Centre back (fold)

Centre front (fold)

Centre front (fold)

Dribbling bib

Fireplace glo

Spectacles case

Patterns for feeding bib, dribbling
bib, collar, fireplace glove, spectacles
case, egg cosy and pot holders are
without seams.

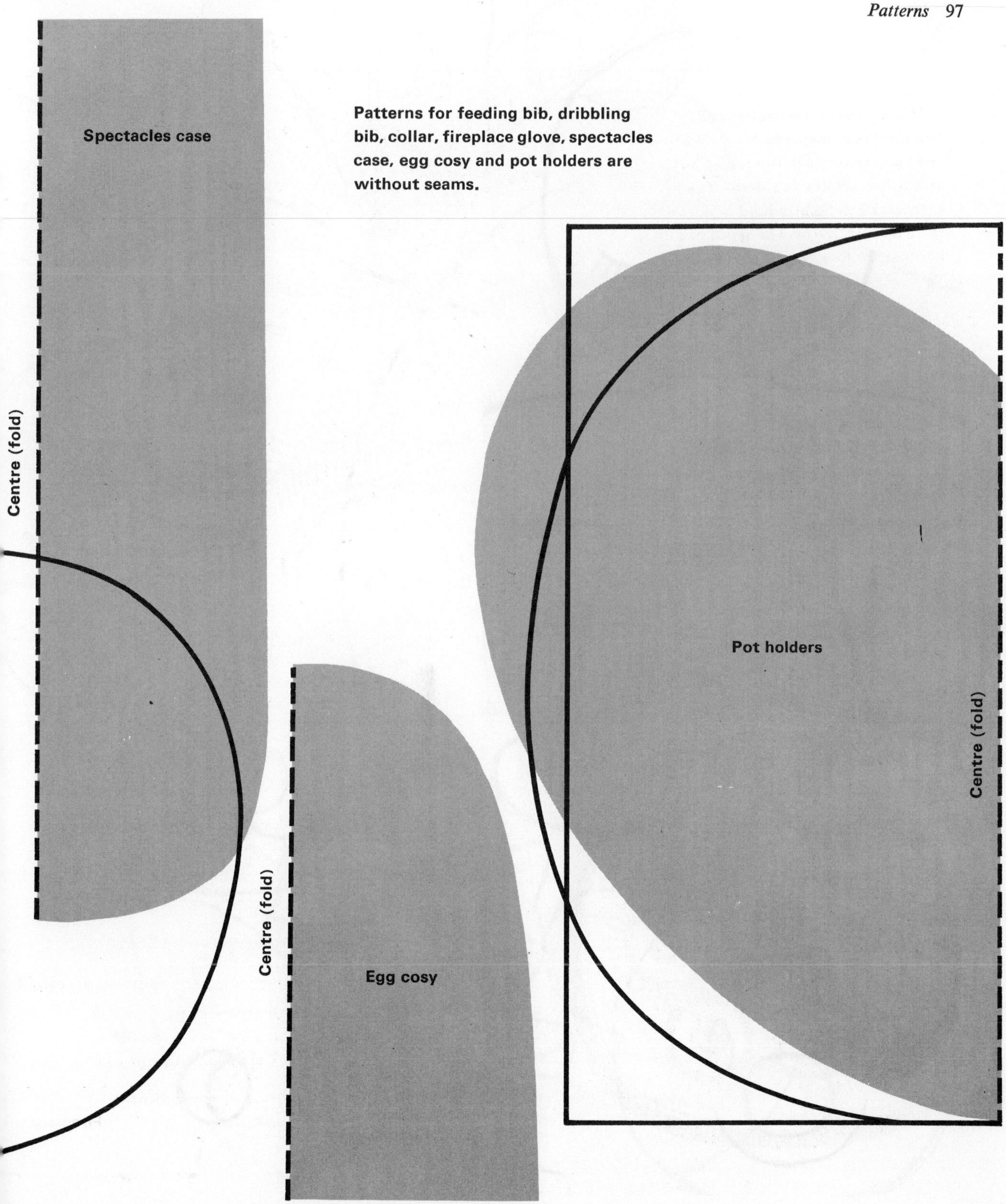

Centre (fold)

Centre (fold)

Pot holders

Centre (fold)

Egg cosy

1. This shows circles in various stitches. You need not draw all the lines and dots on to the fabric but only a few circles as shown. The examples can be arranged in a row for a border, in rows beneath one another, or in a ring; see pages 16-21.

2. Pattern for the felt embroidery on page 57.

3. Pattern for the flower embroidery on page 14. Look at the colour photograph for stitches and colours used. The yarn is embroidery wool.

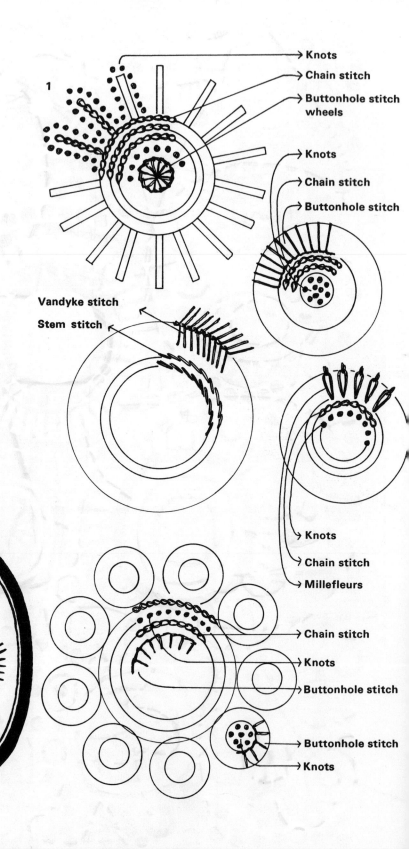

1

→ Knots
→ Chain stitch
→ Buttonhole stitch wheels
→ Knots
→ Chain stitch
→ Buttonhole stitch

Vandyke stitch

Stem stitch

→ Knots
→ Chain stitch
→ Millefleurs

→ Chain stitch
→ Knots
→ Buttonhole stitch
→ Buttonhole stitch
→ Knots

2

3

**Patterns for
felt dolls
on page 54**

Clown's shoe

Tail for large cat

Clown

Body

Dress

Centre front and back

Cat

Teddy bear

Small cat

Tail

Hawaiian girl

Pattern for the houses on page 13

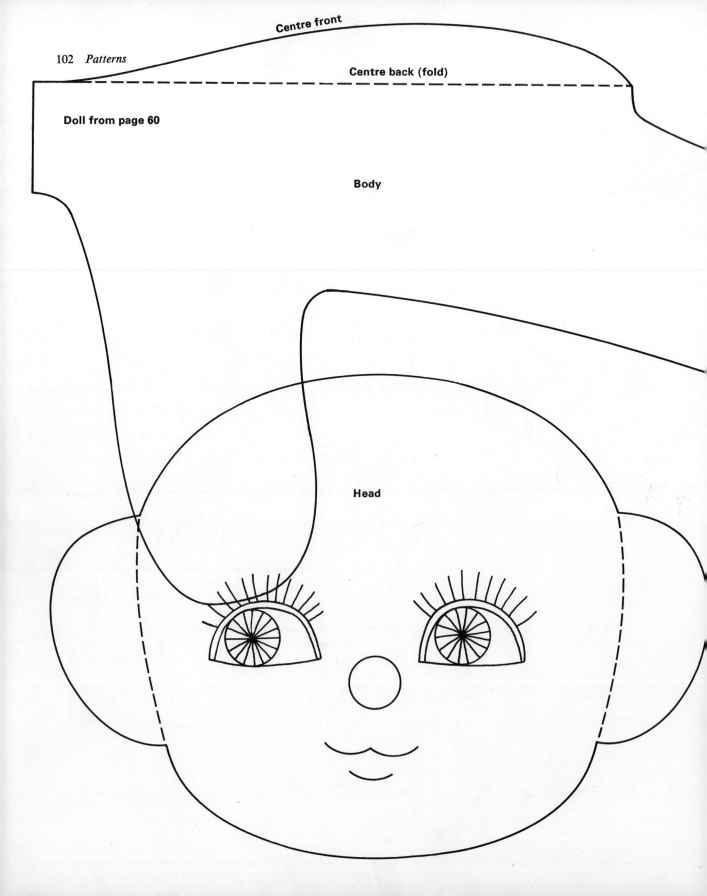

Centre front

Centre back (fold)

Doll from page 60

Body

Head

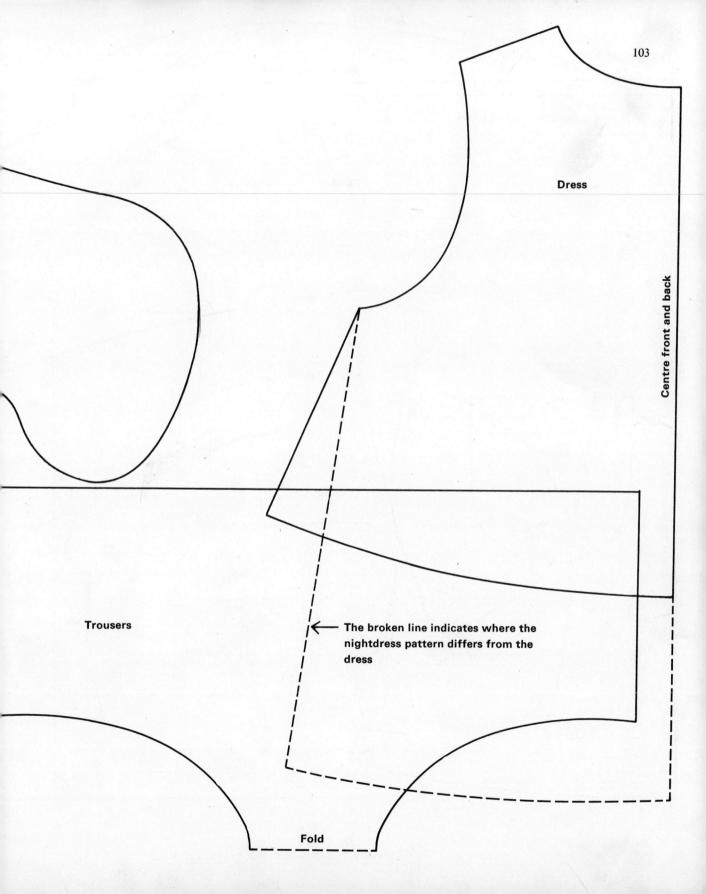

Dress

Centre front and back

Trousers

← The broken line indicates where the nightdress pattern differs from the dress

Fold

Patterns for doll's clothes on pages 60-63

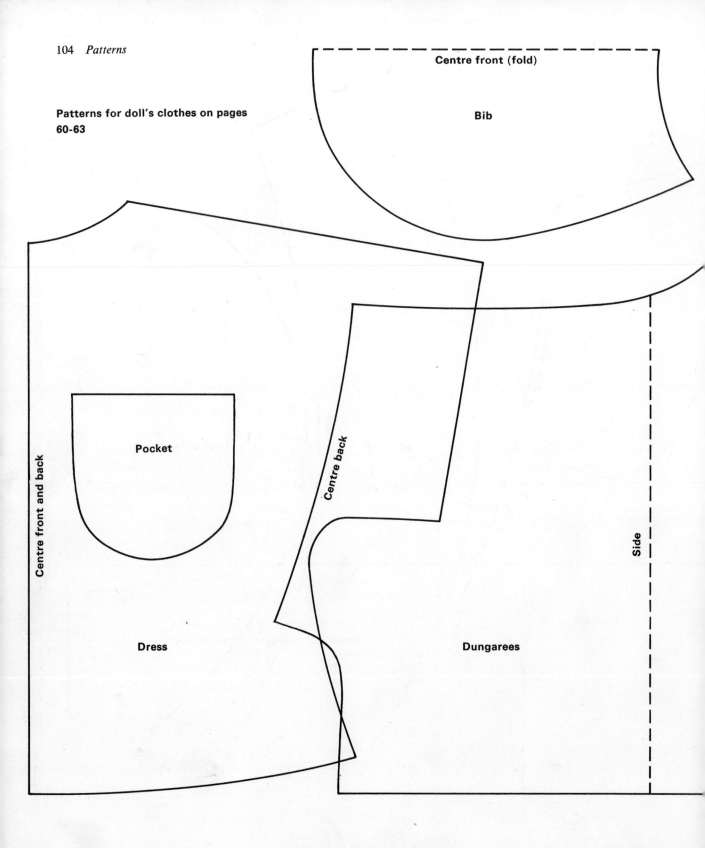

Centre front (fold)

Bib

Centre front and back

Pocket

Centre back

Side

Dress

Dungarees

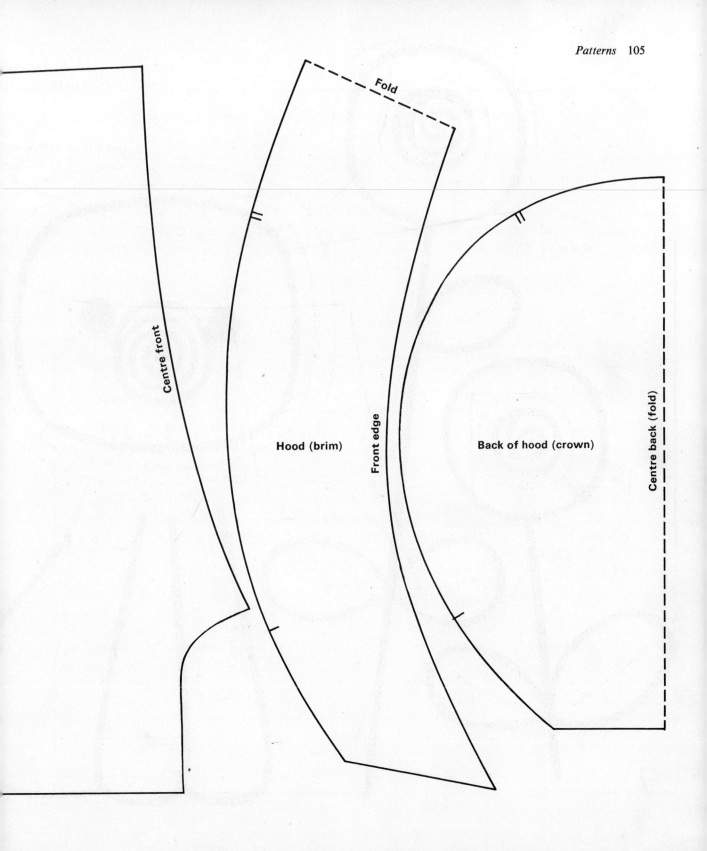

Fold

Centre front

Hood (brim)

Front edge

Back of hood (crown)

Centre back (fold)

Patterns for pictures of lion an
cushion on pages 64-65

→ 3 rows of Rya wor

Rya work

Rya work

Rya loops of fishing line

Couching

String

Rya work

Rya work

Pattern for cord embroidery on page 69

Pattern for bird on page 42

Pattern for fish on page 42

Pattern for tree on page 42

**Patterns for flower, snail and tiger
picture on page 41**

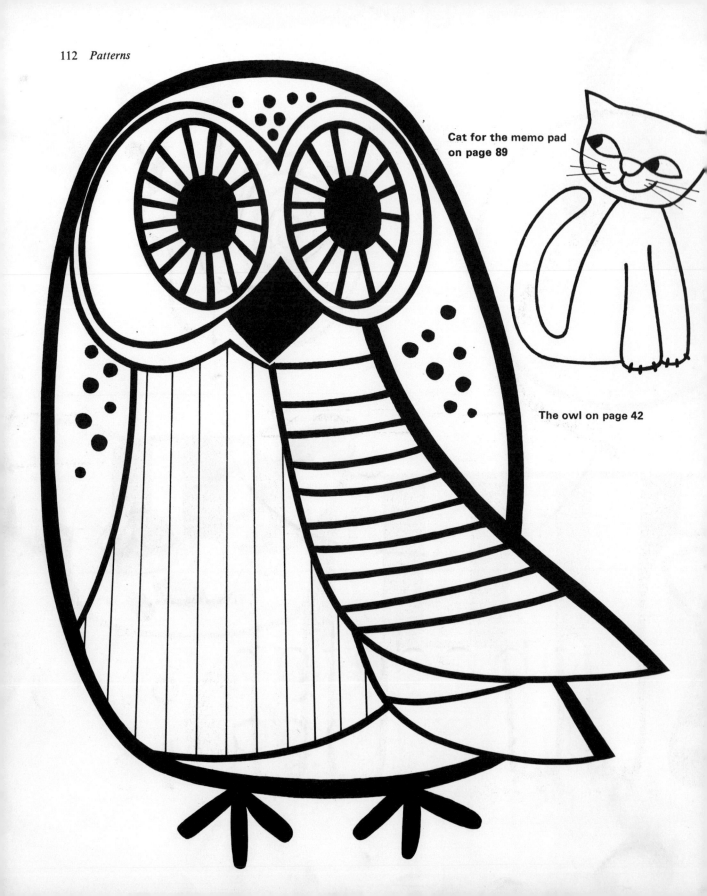

Cat for the memo pad
on page 89

The owl on page 42

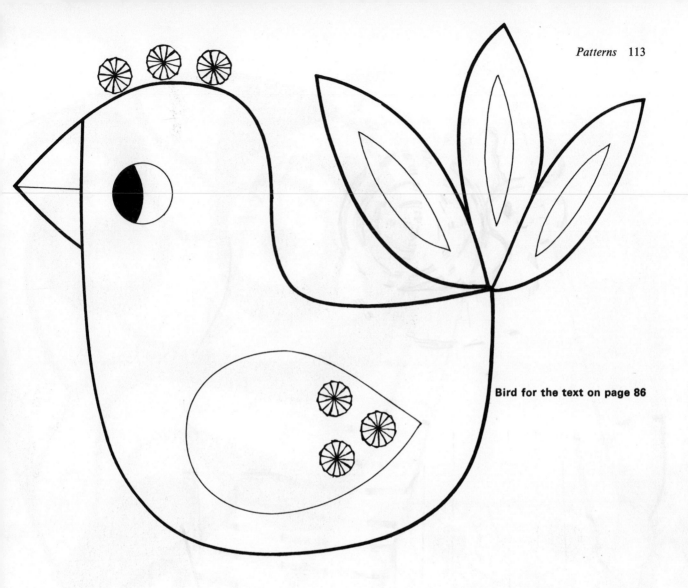

Bird for the text on page 86

Letters for nameplates on page 85

abcdefgh ijklmnopq rstuvwxyz

Pattern for the
clown on page 24

Pattern for the
fish on page 79

Pattern for the purse on page 79

Patterns for Christmas carpet on page 48

Christmas tree

Snowman

Flower

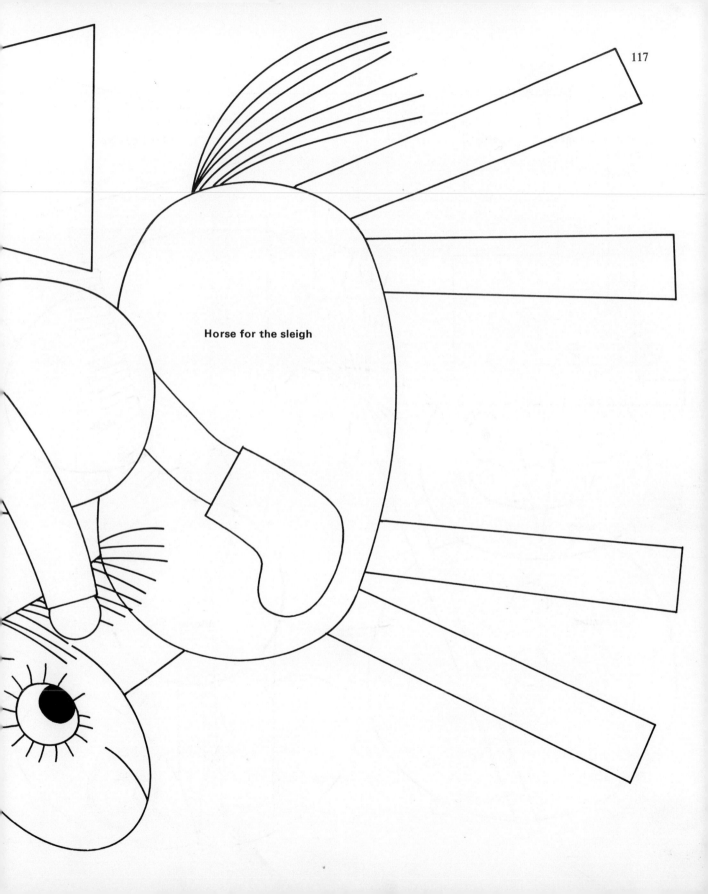

Horse for the sleigh

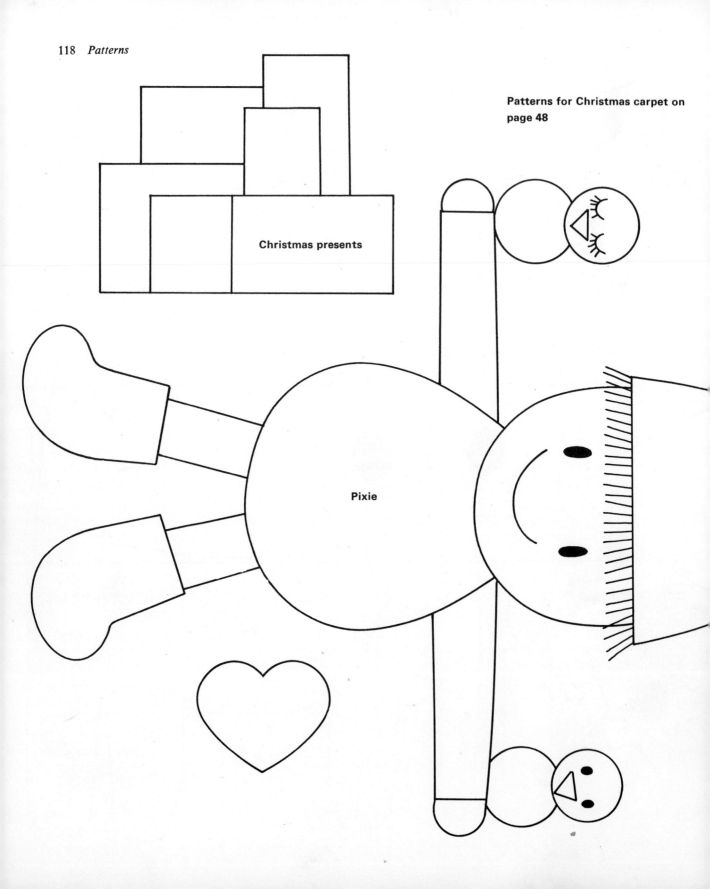

Christmas presents

Patterns for Christmas carpet on
page 48

Pixie

Cat

Cat

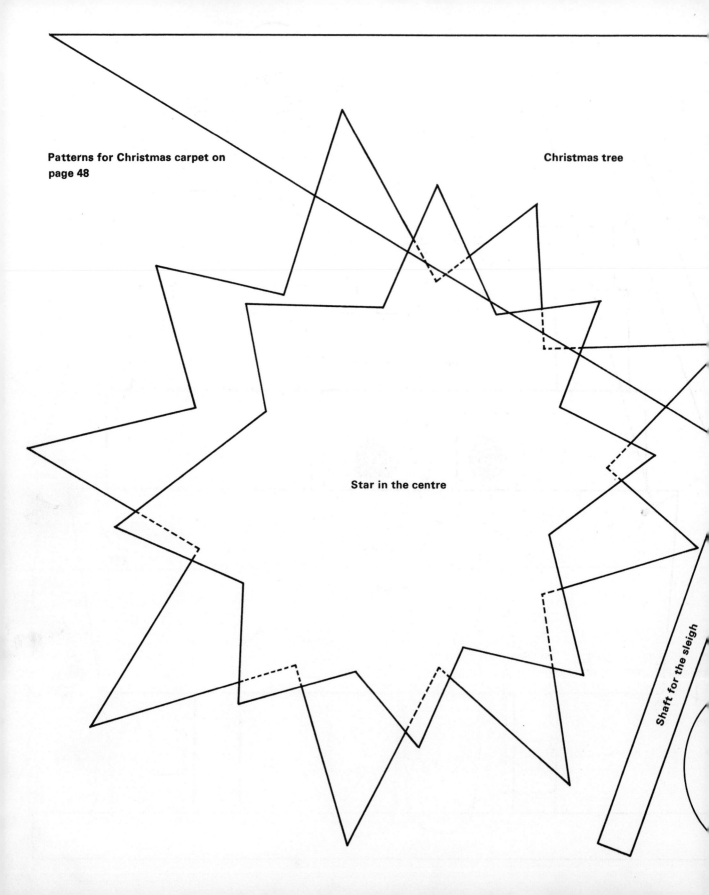

Patterns for Christmas carpet on
page 48

Christmas tree

Star in the centre

Shaft for the sleigh

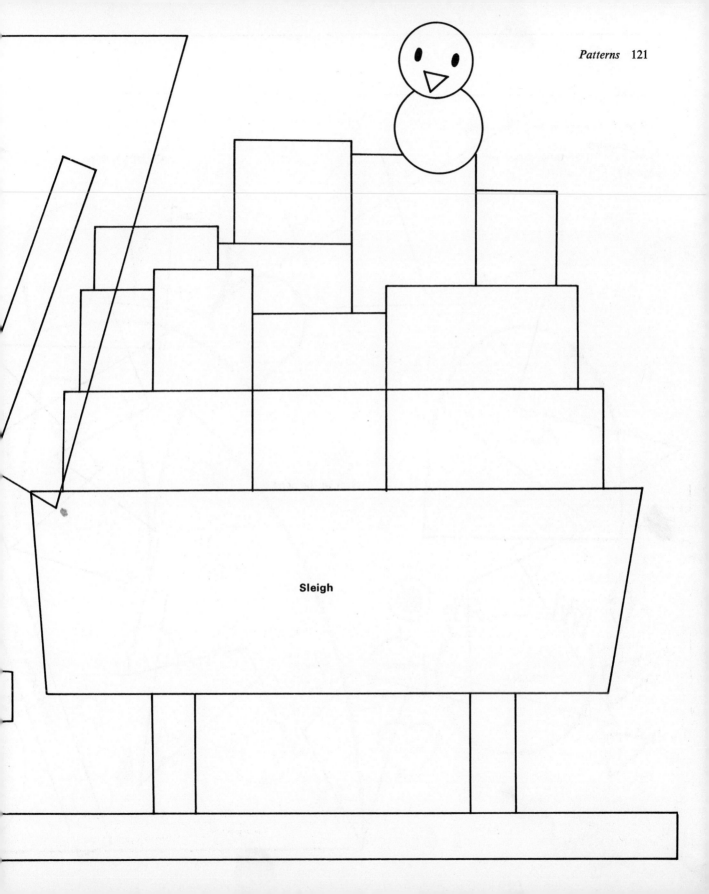

Sleigh

**Pattern for Easter hen with chicks
on page 80**

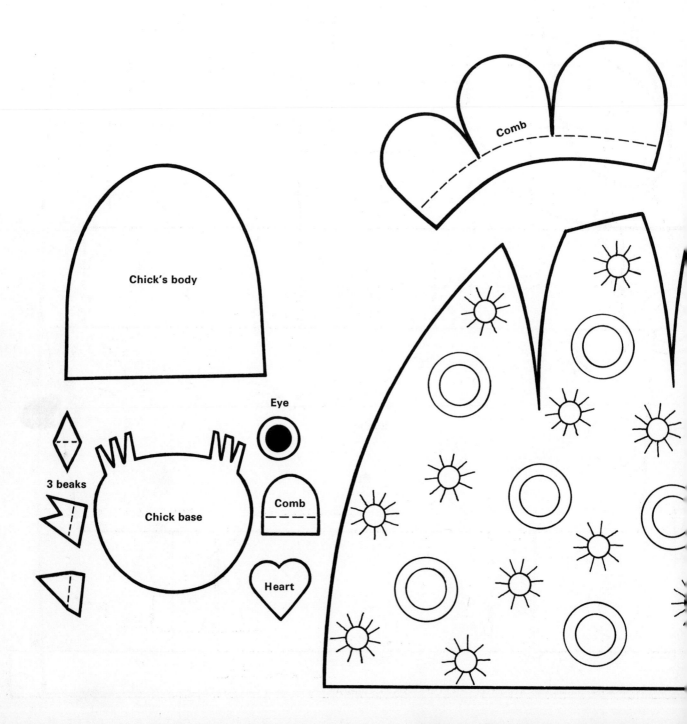

Comb

Chick's body

Eye

3 beaks

Chick base

Comb

Heart

Beak

Wattle

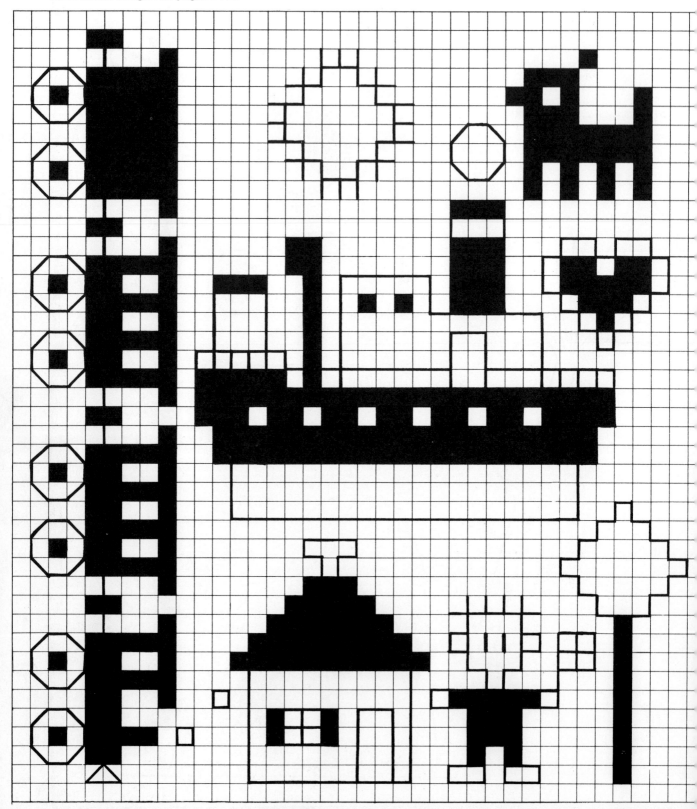

Decoration for fireplace glove on
pages 57 and 83

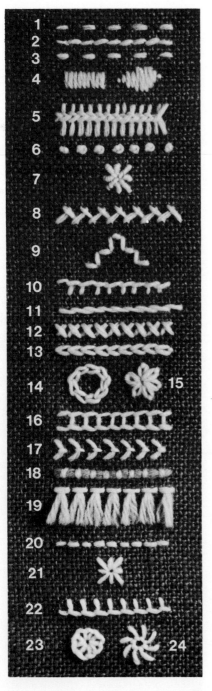

LIST OF STITCHES

The illustration on the left shows the various stitches in the following sequence:

1. Running stitch
2. Double running stitch
3. Tacking (or running stitch)
4. Satin stitch
5. Vandyke stitch
6. French knots
7. Bullion knots
8. Herring-bone stitch
9. Holbein stitch
10. Blanket stitch
11. Stem stitch
12. Cross stitch
13. Chain stitch
14. Chain stitch in rings
15. Millefleurs
16. Open chain stitch
17. Fly stitch
18. Couching
19. Rya work
20. Back stitch
21. Star
22. Buttonhole stitch
23. Buttonhole stitch wheel
24. Another variation of buttonhole stitch

LIST OF SUPPLIERS

Most of the materials in this book can be obtained from specialist embroidery shops and the needlework departments of large stores. Only a few addresses are given below and it should be stressed that these are not by any means the only firms which supply materials for embroidery work.

The following stock most embroidery requirements and will accept postal orders:

The Needlewoman Shop
146-148 Regent Street
London, W1A 6BA

Mace & Nairn
89 Crane Street
Salisbury
Wiltshire

Dryad Ltd
Northgates
Leicester, LE1 4QR

Glenshee Fabrics are excellent for embroidery. They can be obtained from good embroidery shops, but should you experience any difficulty you can write to the manufacturers for the address of your nearest stockist:

Richmond Brothers
Balfield Road Works
Dundee, DD3 6AJ

For a wide range of sequins:

Ells & Farrier Ltd
5 Princes Street
Hanover Square
London, W1R 8PH

INDEX